OTHER BOOKS BY
REINHOLD NIEBUHR

———

REFLECTIONS ON THE END OF
AN ERA

REFLECTIONS ON THE END OF AN ERA

By

Reinhold Niebuhr

CHARLES SCRIBNER'S SONS

NEW YORK · LONDON

1934

HB
501
.N5
cop.2

TO MY BROTHER
H. RICHARD NIEBUHR

PREFACE

THE following reflections are merely tracts for the times. They deal with questions which deserve more systematic treatment than are accorded to them in these pages. If their publication is justified at all the justification must be found in the urgency of the issues which our generation faces. The basic conviction which runs through them is that the liberal culture of modernity is quite unable to give guidance and direction to a confused generation which faces the disintegration of a social system and the task of building a new one. In my opinion adequate spiritual guidance can come only through a more radical political orientation and more conservative religious convictions than are comprehended in the culture of our era. The effort to combine political radicalism with a more classical and historical interpretation of religion will strike the modern mind as bizarre and capricious. It will satisfy neither the liberals in politics and religion, nor the political radicals nor the devotees of traditional Christianity. These reflections are therefore presented without much hope that they will elicit any general concurrence. Perhaps they will help a little to shake the easy faith by which modern liberalism lives and through which the actual and tragic facts of contemporary history are, in the opinion of the present writer, obscured.

I would like to express my gratitude to my wife, whose criticisms are responsible for the elimination of many flaws in words and thoughts in the manuscript of this book; and to my brother, Professor H. Richard Niebuhr, who disagrees with most of the conclusion at which I arrive, but whose stimulating analyses of the contemporary religious and social problem prompted many of these reflections.

R. N.

UNION THEOLOGICAL SEMINARY,
NEW YORK: December, 1933.

CONTENTS

REFLECTIONS ON THE END OF AN ERA

I

THE LIFE AND DEATH
OF CIVILIZATIONS

I

THE LIFE AND DEATH
OF CIVILIZATIONS

IT is a strange irony of history that a commercial
and industrial civilization, which might have
had special reasons for being apprehensive about
its vitality and longevity, should have been particularly optimistic. A philosophy of unqualified optimism has attended the entire brief reign of modern
capitalism. Destined to premature decay, it dreamed
of progress almost until the hour of its dissolution.

The optimism of modernity has many roots. The
expansive mood of an era, which felt that its conquest
of nature had provided the human race with new and
unlimited possibilities of development; the effect of
the evolutionary theory in biology upon the interpretation of human history; and the confidence of
modern rationalism in the possibility of arresting the
processes of nature by the artifices of mind, all these
have contributed to the unlimited faith in itself of a
commercial civilization. But they are not as basic to
the creed of modern optimism as the unique charac-
teristics of the civilization itself. A commercial and
industrial civilization is mechanical rather than or-

ganic in its structure. Its cement of social cohesion consists of means of production and communication. It is this mechanism which has deceived the prophets and wise men of our era in regard to the actual nature of human life.

Mechanism easily veils the actual realities of life. It makes human life seem to be a series of highly rational social relationships and hides the fact that these relations are actually the product, not of mind and conscience but of power and impulse. The techniques of credit and exchange, of stock ownership, dividends and interest reduce the processes of economic life to seemingly passionless circles and series of social relationships in which reason and conscience have ostensibly eliminated friction and social conflict. The social mechanisms of a commercial civilization, in short, veil the brutal realities of social life and obscure the factors of egoistic and imperial impulse which determine it to a large degree. They prevent the modern man from realizing that collective behavior is primarily impulsive, that its impulses are heedless and undirected and that will-to-live of every individual and social organism is easily transmuted into an imperial will-to-power.

It is the function of reason to relate life to life in terms of harmony. To accomplish this task it must restrain the immediate impulses in the individual which war against each other; and the organized impulses of the individual which set his life against the life of his community; and the impulses of his community which bring it in conflict with the total community of mankind. Ideally reason therefore prevents and reduces social conflict by relating interest to interest and will to will in ever widening circles of social harmony. In such social harmonies various forms of life do not feed upon each other but support each other and death is postponed.

But the dominance of reason over impulse is much more tentative and insecure than modern culture realizes. Frequently, as in the mechanisms of modern civilization, it provides rationalization rather than restraints for the play of egoistic impulse; or it may bring the impulses of an individual in harmony with each other without creating a harmony between the individual and society; or it may give cohesion and direction to the impulses of a limited community without relating that community to the total needs of human life. When reason reduces the anarchy of impulse within a limited area in either individual or social life it may merely construct a more effective force of egoistic impulse which sets itself against the rights and needs of the whole of human life. A high degree of prudence may, for instance, persuade a governing class or a group of imperialistic nations to eliminate anarchy within their ranks in order that they may more effectively keep other classes or races

5

under their dominion. Nor is there any guarantee that a rational force which is strong enough to create limited social harmonies will be strong enough to establish an ultimate harmony of life with life.

Every social organism, whether a dominant social class, a unique organization of society or a peculiar form of culture is endowed with a natural will-to-live. Reason may be the very force which transmutes this will-to-live into a will-to-power. The transmutation is practically inevitable because life in any particular form is darkly conscious of the fact that it is arbitrary and capricious and that competing forms of life are challenging its right to existence. The immediate reaction to this challenge is an effort to overcome its arbitrary and capricious character by universalizing itself and by destroying or subjecting competing forms of life to itself. It thus seeks to postpone or avert death by eliminating other forms of life which challenge its right to existence. Since a peculiar form of life, individual or social, can never conquer the whole of life this imperialistic effort is always self-defeating in the end. It arouses other forms of life to antagonism and creates resentments which finally become the instruments of its own undoing. Thus social organisms always tend to seal the doom of their ultimate destruction in the very act of asserting their vitality and in the effort to avoid the doom of death.

6

Though the rational force in life may be used to organize impulse and transmute it into the imperialistic will-to-power, it must not be assumed that this is the only form in which it expresses itself. In its purest form it continues to create a consciousness of the arbitrary and capricious character of any life-expression and seeks to bring each particular form of individual or social life into terms of unity rather than conflict with other forms. Thus it diminishes the uniqueness of any form of life and tends to extend the narrow will-to-live into a broad affirmation of life itself.

Reason may, in short, result in two conflicting strategies: the strategy of universalizing a particular form of life by seeking to subject all competing forms to itself, and the strategy of subjecting all particular forms of life to the universal. Driven to its logical conclusion the latter strategy ends in the impulse of all high religion to subordinate every specific form of life to life in its more absolute form, to God. In this subjection and subordination there is a more or less conscious or unconscious recognition of the arbitrary, irrational and tentative character of any particular life-expression and a consequent desire to eliminate the peril of death by transforming it into a more absolute form of life. That is why asceticism, a strategy of self-restraint to the very point of self-annihilation, always grows somewhere in the garden of true religion. Self-assertion is felt to be an impertinence before and an affront to the absolute. The effort is therefore made to check its presumption.

Naturally this impulse of pure spirituality comes in conflict with the will-to-live with which all nature is endowed, and which seeks the perpetuation of life in any immediate form in which it has been able to come to an expression. On the level of pure impulse this will-to-live expresses itself in merely defensive terms. Even the predatory animal of fields and forests usually destroys other life only in order to preserve its own. But when the impulses of self-preservation are mixed with reason and a form of life grows more self-conscious the will-to-live develops into the will-to-power. Its higher degree of self-consciousness increases the fear of death and extinction; and reason persuades it to anticipate the peril of death from opposing forms of life by destroying these competing forces or by bringing them into harmless servitude to it. (Servitude may, incidentally, be a more successful form of imperialism than the annihilation of the foe. Primitive tribes destroyed their foes and the more advanced ones enslaved them, having discovered that a living foe in servitude is a more potent means of aggrandizement than a dead foe.) Imperialism is thus an inevitable concomitant of the more conscious types of the impulse of self-preservation.

8

No stable equilibrium is ever reached in history between the two impulses: the impulse to subject the individual or social ego to the universal even to the point of self-annihilation or absorption and the impulse to universalize the ego even to the point of destroying or enslaving all competing forms of life. If the conflict between these two forms of rationality is roughly defined in these pages as the conflict between "nature" and "spirit" it must be borne in mind that these two terms are mythological rather than scientific descriptions of the facts. The imperialistic force in life is not pure nature because imperialism arises only when natural impulses are directed and organized by mind. The ethical force in life is termed "spirit" rather than "reason" because some of the force which impels men to affirm the life of the other rather than their own life is derived not from reason but from natural impulse. Yet it is through reason that these altruistic impulses are carried beyond the limits set by nature.[1]

[1]C. G. Jung, in his recent book, *Modern Man in Search of a Soul,* writes: "I do not doubt that the natural instincts are forces of propulsion in human life, whether we call them sexuality or the will-to-power; but I also do not doubt that these forces come into collision with the spirit for they are continually colliding with something and why should that something not be called spirit? I am far from knowing what spirit is in itself and equally far from knowing what instincts are. The one is as mysterious as the other yet I am unable to dismiss the one by explaining it in terms of the other," p. 136.

I find in this analysis a substantiation of the sharp distinction between "spirit" and "nature" which I desire to make in these pages; and also a parallel for my failure to define these mythological conceptions in precise scientific terms.

In the life of individuals the ethical impulse, though it fails to check egoism to the degree assumed possible in modern culture, does nevertheless bring the impulse of imperialism under restraint. In human collectives and social groups the imperial impulse is clearly the most dominant. Since the life of a nation, a race or a class seems, from the perspective of the individuals who compose it, to be the very universal life and value to which individual life ought to be subordinated, it is inevitable that much of the force of "spirit" in life should be wasted in covering the arbitrary and partial forms of social life with the aura of the absolute. That is why religion, which is always a source or consequence of the ethical impulse in individual life, frequently becomes a dangerous source of moral confusion in the larger social relations. Nations and classes, cultures and civilization are usually able to use religion, not to reveal the imperfection and partiality of their life and values, but to give the prestige of the absolute to what is relative and tentative.

It is the peculiar defect of a trading and commercial civilization that it is more than ordinarily confused in estimating the power of the imperial impulse in life. The trader and the industrial oligarch are, unlike the rulers of previous civilizations, not in organic relation to the impulses of nature in man. The oligarchs of other civilizations carried the sword and used it. They accepted warfare as the rule of life, gloried in its romance and accepted its victories and defeats as belonging to life's inevitable vicissitudes. The modern oligarch conducts a bank or a factory. He "serves" mankind. All bloodshed is abhorrent to him. The lust of power and the imperial impulse may prompt his actions but they express themselves subconsciously rather than consciously. He is not fully conscious of life's brutalities. He may tenderly send his family to escape the winter's cold on the sands of Palm Beach while his workers starve to death amid the social confusion of an economic depression. His cities are filled with humanitarians who eat meat but regard the killing of animals with repulsion. His institutions of learning boast of academics, supported by rather generous crumbs which fall from the rich man's table, who invent schemes for saving modern civilization by transmuting it into a rational and moral accommodation of interest to interest in which all coercion and conflict will be avoided. They are unconscious of the fact that they are dreaming of such a moral world in a leisure provided by privileges which have emerged out of a terrific conflict of power.

The self-deception of the academics is derived from a special kind of detachment from the inertia and brutality of impulsive life peculiar to the learned man. This deception is not new in history. But the modern man of power is living under illusions which his predecessors did not have in the same degree. He is unconsciously driven by the lust of power, as all strong men are. But he thinks that he is merely engaged in the business of manufacturing drain pipes or floating bond issues or saving backward nations by lending them money at 8 per cent. These industrial and financial transactions are mechanical. The processes by which they are accomplished are abstracted from the fears and hatreds, the lusts and passions, which really move human life. They seem therefore to be supremely rational and delude those who engage in them. The business men are even capable of suggesting, when the actual conflict of impulse reveals itself in the political world, that this conflict could be avoided if they, rather than the politicians, could only take charge of politics.

Thus a capitalistic period of society was ushered in by a philosophy of liberalism, the economics of *laissez-faire* and the ethics of utilitarianism. The common note in all of these viewpoints was that life was to be made secure and the social structure was to be made permanent by a rational and prudent adjustment of life to life. According to the theory of Adam Smith, the self-interest of competing individuals would automatically make for social harmony. According to the utilitarians, social harmony would be achieved if the force of self-interest were to be qualified by a prudence which knew how to include the general interest in the self-interest. In either case the force of egoism was not regarded as a peril to social harmony. Thus a world was envisaged in which all nations and classes would live together in perfect reciprocity. The nations in such a world would not place tariff restrictions upon world trade because it was obviously rational to buy goods where they could be secured at the lowest rates and to sell them where they would bring the highest price. The characteristic dream of the trader thus became the basis for a whole philosophy of life and history. The world which it envisaged was one in which self-interest was either no peril at all or in which reason would quickly bring the potential anarchy of competing egoisms under control.

The dream of the eighteenth and nineteenth centuries was that of a social order moving from strength to strength and grace to grace. It would never be imperilled by death because it would never arouse competing life to a sanguinary struggle. In it nations were to be related to nations in harmless reciprocity and within each nation the strong would serve the weak because they had realized that they could thus serve their own interests best. This dream was one which grew naturally out of the illusions of traders and academics. Neither class understood the power and persistence of irrational egoism in human behavior, particularly in collective human behavior.

13

The mechanistic and impersonal relations of the trader's civilization supported the rationalistic illusions of academics. Together they gave us a moral culture built upon the quicksands of prudential self-interest and a philosophy of life which understands neither the heights to which life may rise nor the depths to which it may sink. The whole tragic conflict between the ethical and the imperial force in life is effaced in a theory which does superficial justice to both. That is how the liberal culture of modernity is defective in both religious profundity and political sagacity. An adequate religion develops only where the ethical impulse is set in vivid juxtaposition to the forces of nature in man; and man is forced both to seek after an impossible victory and to adjust himself to an inevitable defeat. An adequate politics is possible only if the task of achieving some kind of decent harmony in social relations is essayed with a clear understanding of the stubborn inertia which every social purpose meets in the egoism of individuals and groups.

With rather pathetic irony modern civilization proceeded to tear itself asunder in its conflicts between nations and classes while modern culture dreamed of perpetual peace. The trader is not a conscious imperialist; but he needs raw products for his machines, markets for his goods and investment opportunities for his surplus capital. Each modern industrial nation was therefore forced into imperialism; and its imperialism came in conflict with that of other nations, driven by the same necessities. The very reason that each of the modern nations was forced to be excessively imperialistic was due to the fact that the dominant economic groups in each of them would not divide the benefits of the productive process with the masses sufficiently to provide markets for the process within the boundaries of each nation. It is instructive that during the period of decay in this system of production a world economic conference should be held in which each nation insisted on the necessity of freer trade between the nations while every nation continued to raise tariff barriers and to seek trade advantages in depreciated currencies in the vain effort to sell the world more goods than it was willing to buy from the world. It is significant too that the ultimate disintegration of such a civilization should be foreshadowed by rising nationalistic passions which defy the attempted international control of the League of Nations, the one achievement (or was it gesture?) of the liberal spirit of the era.

The hope of harmony between the classes has been as cruelly disappointed as the liberal dream of international reciprocity. The mechanical civilization of the commercial and industrial oligarch tends to fall apart not only internationally but intra-nationally. The class struggle is indeed as old as history;

but in other ages personal relations and organic societies tended to mitigate and to obscure the force of
class antagonisms. It remained for a social order
which hoped for a perfect mutuality of interest between social classes to generate the most venomous
and destructive class antagonisms. No feudal squire
ever beat down his rebellious serfs more ruthlessly
than the industrial oligarch does when he finds his
reign imperilled by the men who run his machines
without respect for or loyalty to his power.

Thus a social order which imagined that it could
easily adjust life to life and interest to interest is
destined to end in terrible conflicts in which class and
national antagonisms express themselves in bewilder-
ing confusion. The moral superficiality of modern
culture betrayed it into an easy faith that reason
had conquered or could conquer and restrain the anarchic impulses which express themselves in man-as-
nature. It had not realized that reason may be used
much more easily to justify impulse and to invent instruments for its efficacious expression than to check
and restrain impulse. That was a fatal mistake because it permitted a more unrestrained expression
of impulse than ever before in history.

Every age and every dominant class has its own hy-
pocrisies by which it justifies its impulses. But the
illusions and deceptions of a liberal culture have been
particularly flagrant because it has been so complete-

ly oblivious to the anarchic, the demonic and the primeval in man's collective behavior. Therefore an age of liberalism, rationalism and optimism is ushered to its close by a World War which can be distinguished from previous conflicts, chiefly by the effectiveness of its lethal instruments, the universality of its destruction and the superior plausibility of its various moral justifications.

The wise men of our era did not realize at all that mind is the servant of impulse before it becomes its master and that the first effect of mind upon impulse is to make man more deadly in his lusts than the brute. Impulses always express themselves in well-defined limits in nature. There are therefore inchoate harmonies in nature's anarchies. There is anarchy in the forest; for each species lives by robbing and destroying other life. Yet there is also harmony; for each species survives. But in man reason bursts the bonds and limits which nature sets upon her own impulses. Man's higher degree of self-consciousness and egocentricity transmutes the brute's will-to-survive into the human will-to-power. If the simple individual, as for instance the peasant of Germany or France, should lack the will-to-power, it will not be absent from the character of those who construct the power of leadership out of the guileless loyalties of these simple individuals nor from the national and other human groups which compound the fears pro-

ceeding from the impulse of survival in individuals into a national will-to-power. A nation's desire to
dominate is always justified by its statesmen as a
strategy of defense; and this justification always has
a measure of legitimacy, from an immediate perspective, because power seems to be the only protection
against extinction.

Thus the enterprises of collective man, his social
orders, his empires and civilizations, must die a
sanguinary death. They cannot "die in bed" nor let
senility take its course. They combine the robust
will-to-live of nature with conscious man's pathetic
discovery that the "best defense is an attack"
and that the exercise of dominion is one method
of escaping extinction. Therefore every social system, faced by the peril of death, is bound to make one
final and ruthless effort to avert its doom by destroying or suppressing competing forms of life. In the
history of every declining monarchial system a period
can be found in which the challenge of democratic
forms was met by a futile effort to make the monarchy
more absolute. After the same manner a declining
capitalistic economic system is bound to meet the
threat of socialist alternatives with a final effort to
purify capitalism of concessions made to its competing economic forms and to maintain it by sheer force
against its foes. Inevitably such an effort must result in aggravating the injustices which have sapped

18

the vitality of the social order and in increasing the vehemence with which its victims will resist those injustices. Thus a dying social order hastens its death in the frantic effort to avoid or postpone it.

II

PROPHECY OF DOOM

PROPHECY OF DOOM

THE contemporary situation in the economic and political life of the western world is a perfect illustration of the pathetic inability of senile social systems to mend the error of their ways. Our western society is obviously in the process of disintegration. It lives under the peril of a new war which it seems powerless to avert and it suffers from serious dislocations in its economic processes which it cannot overcome. Though it is generally known that another war will prove suicidal to the whole of western culture it is no longer certain that fear of the possibility of such a suicide will avert the war. The Disarmament Conference has failed to stop the race in armaments which will make such a war both more inevitable and more deadly. It is equally well known that the economic ills of our society cannot be eliminated if wealth is not more equitably distributed. But this knowledge does not result in new social policies which guarantee the more equitable distribution of wealth.

Our knowledge fails us because we are not dealing with a functional ill which might be corrected by a slight change in policy or program. The sickness from which modern civilization suffers is organic and constitutional. It is not due to an incidental defect in the mechanism of production or distribution but to the very character of the social system. The system provides for the private ownership of the productive processes upon which the health of the whole civilization depends. Private ownership means social power; and the unequal distribution of social power leads automatically to inequality and injustice. By vesting the power of ownership in the hands of comparatively few individuals the present social system insures the faulty distribution of the wealth which modern machines create.

Mass production requires mass consumption; and capitalism is unable to provide mass consumption. From this basic ill of modern society all other defects seem to spring. Most of them are derived from the effort to escape the consequences of the fundamental difficulty without eliminating it. Thus, for instance, the natural rivalry between nations is accentuated by a social system which results in overproduction in each nation and forces the nations to seek a market for their surplus in other nations without granting the other nations reciprocal market rights. The consumption capacity of the masses cannot be raised sufficiently to obviate this difficulty within the terms of the capitalistic order; for a more equitable distribution of wealth would ultimately destroy the power of the owners in modern society.

The industrial and financial oligarchs recognise the incompatibility between their actions and the necessities of an interdependent technical age. They therefore demand an international economic conference which will eliminate or mitigate this economic anarchy. But such a conference failed, when it was held, and its failure was inevitable. The international reciprocity at which it aimed would have been possible only if each nation could achieve a higher degree of social and economic mutuality within its boundaries than the private ownership of the productive process permits.

It was not immediately apparent, when the reign of the modern industrialist began in the middle of the past century, that a high degree of social and economic equality would be required to preserve the health of an industrial civilization. The whole world was hungry for the goods which the new machines produced and for more machines to produce more goods. Profits could therefore always be reinvested in enlarging the productive equipment; and excess products could be sold to nations in which the new industry had not yet developed. It was even possible to give credibility to the myth that excessive profits were society's rewards to "abstemious" individuals who restrained their desire to consume goods for the sake of providing capital investments for production. If any moral quality attached to this alleged restraint in consumption it applied only to the capitalists of the first generation. Once the owners became the beneficiaries of the huge profits of modern industry they could reinvest their "earnings" without the slightest diminution of generous living standards. Unable to spend all they earned they could nevertheless claim special moral recognition and economic compensation for not spending it.

The period in which the economic inequality inherent in capitalism did not reveal itself as a source of anarchy and disintegration, was however very brief. The industrial nations were almost under the immediate necessity of extending their political authority in order to insure free access to the raw products which their machines required and security for their investments in foreign lands. Capitalism did not create imperialism; for imperialism is the natural concomitant of the will-to-live of a powerful nation. But capitalism did give a new fillip to the imperialism of strong nations and it accentuated the rivalry between various strong nations for the right to exploit the backward portions of the world. Thus the World War was partially due to the competition of various European nations for the spoils of Africa.

The anarchy of competing imperialisms may be regarded as the childhood disease of capitalism. It was relatively innocuous compared to the later difficulties of glutted markets and over-production. Imperial expansion provided only a very brief moment of respite from the consequences of unequal distribution of wealth. The industrially advanced nations sold not only consumers' goods but machines to the undeveloped nations and they sold not only in cash exchange but on credit, since they were forced to sell more than they bought. As a result they gradually destroyed their markets. Either the other nations began to produce goods themselves with the machines they had acquired, in which case they no longer required the manufactured goods of the more advanced nations; or the service charges on their debt restricted their capacity to buy more goods. Thus China, the British Colonies, Poland, Czecho-Slovakia, Russia and even India are becoming industrialized and the tempo of their industrialization is constantly increasing. The markets of the still purely agrarian nations are restricted almost as much as those of the industrially advancing nations because their wealth production has remained fairly stable while the charges which they must pay on past debts have constantly increased. The technique of providing markets for both surplus products and surplus capital by lending surplus capital to permit the purchase of surplus goods has run its course in both English and American imperialism in less than a century. Capitalism

27

in short can exist only by attempting to universalize itself but it can live healthily only as long as it fails to do so. The more its system of wealth production and unequal distribution spreads throughout the world the more untenable it becomes. No better illustration could be found in history of the paradox that the seed of death is in the thrust of life.

If the anarchy of conflicting imperialisms, symbolized by the World War, represented the childhood disease of capitalism, the surfeited markets of the present moment, symbolized by the world depression, may be regarded as a revelation of its senility. The former resulted from a clash between the youthful and still vigorous national wills of the industrial nations. The latter is a consequence of the simultaneous stagnation of the economic processes in the same nations. The maldistribution of wealth is the basic cause of both. The very brief period of a decade and a half between the World War and the world depression is a rather accurate symbol of the brevity of the capitalistic order. Here, as in other instances of human history, the excesses of a robust youth have aggravated the diseases of age. The burden of war debts increased the economic dislocations of western economy and further restricted the buying power of the multitudes.

There is a pathetic irony in the fact that the world depression is postponing the catastrophe toward which our civilization is drifting and yet making it more inevitable; for the poverty of the nations accentuates national animosities and yet postpones hostilities. The nations are too poor to fight but their very poverty increases their competition for world markets and tempts them to engage in desperate efforts to exclude each other from their own markets. Such efforts have the seed of war in them.

The real tragedy of our contemporary situation is that modern technology has made social mutuality and international reciprocity an absolute imperative, a very law of survival; while our system of economic ownership makes both intra-national justice and international reciprocity impossible. The obvious character of our need and the urgency of our obligation to be more mutual tempt our wise men to optimism. They imagine that we will certainly not fail to do what so patently needs to be done. "If this is all the trouble" (the maldistribution of wealth), declares Mr. H. G. Wood blandly in a recent book, "capitalists should be intelligent enough to avert disaster."[1] This kind of optimism is derived from an uncritical rationalism which assumes that men who are moved by interest are able to see the obvious facts of history and that they invariably obey the imperatives which the facts disclose. It fails to recog-

[1] H. G. Wood, *Christianity and Communism* (English title, *The Truth and Error of Communism*), 1933.

29

nize with what stubborn inertia and blindness men will pursue their own interests even if these are proved to be in conflict with a more general interest. Our modern optimists do not understand that the Pauline confession, "The good which I would I do not: but the evil which I would not, that I do," is perennially justified by human experience, particularly in collective human behavior. A social or political system, a ruling class or an economic organization may be persuaded to mend some of its incidental defects; but it can hardly be persuaded to recognize that its day is done. If the social injustice which makes modern capitalism untenable is actually rooted in the very nature of capitalism it is not likely that capitalism will be converted to justice by logical and historical proof that social inequality will destroy it. The wiser and more sensitive spirits in a ruling oligarchy may deprecate injustice and seek to mitigate it, but even they will not find it easy to admit that social injustice springs inevitably from their type of social power.

If, as seems to be the case, the necessities of a technical age are incompatible with the inequality inherent in the private ownership of the productive process, our learned men are wrong in assuming that the recognition of this incompatibility will persuade the beneficiaries of a system of private ownership to abdicate their power, or even that they will acquiesce peacefully in its abrogation. If they follow the impulses of nature and the example of previous ruling castes they will fight to the end to maintain power and privileges which the logic of history has proved untenable.

Our optimistic rationalists fail to recognize that the collective enterprises of man belong to the order of nature much more than to the order of reason. The parable of the jungle gives a much truer picture of the life and death of civilizations than those usually devised by rationalists and moralists. In the jungle life feeds on life until it is itself destroyed. In the same way the predatory character of every social system is the ultimate cause of its dissolution. History is the oft-repeated tale of a once robust life coming to an ignominious death. Civilizations, like men and beasts, perish partly because they grow old and feeble and partly because they are slain by those whose enmity they have deserved by their ruthlessness.

There is a profound truth in the religious insight which ascribes death to sin: "The wages of sin is death." The judgment is not wholly true; for senility as well as sin causes death. Every organism in nature has its apportioned day and sinks into dust when its day is done. That applies to social organisms as much as to biological ones. Yet in the specific instance death is not frequently due to senility alone. Senility is only a contributory cause. What is most robust in social history as well as in field and forest lives at the expense of other life and dies when it can no longer protect itself against the enmity which its predatory life has prompted. Since death in history and in nature comes by senility as well as sin all purely moralistic interpretations of history are mistaken. A social system simply outlives its usefulness; and its temper and tempo, its presuppositions and organizations fail to meet the requirements of a new situation. It must therefore give way to a new social system which is better fitted to organize life under new conditions. Yet all life, in both nature and history, is driven by immediate impulses to an egoism which is incompatible with the ultimate requirements of survival. It therefore perishes because of its "sin." Thus every social system develops disproportions of power and privilege, greater than any rule of justice would sanction and dangerous to its own longevity. Yet the injustices which result in the premature death of a social system are also the expression of its vitality. To invite the oligarchies which rule every society to live by the law of justice is equivalent to requesting the oligarchs to abdicate; for there is always an element of sheer power in their rule which must appear as a capricious and irrational element from a purely rational perspective.

In the vital period of a social system the pretensions

and exactions of power do not appear to be irrational and unjust because they actually succeed in organizing society and they participate in the reverence which common men give to the organization of life about them. But when a given oligarchy, with its particular type of power, fails to preserve the orderly functions of society its injustices become both more apparent and more insufferable. Its exactions arouse resentments partly because they are no longer taken for granted, as the natural price which men must pay for the boon of orderly government, and partly because they actually become increasingly unbearable. Thus the rise of modern commerce made the anarchies of the military rule of feudal lords impossible and the further development of commerce and industry must make the rule, and the attendant anarchies, of the modern economic overlords untenable.

When a given type of oligarchy fails to preserve the orderly processes of society and suffers from loss of prestige and reverence, the wise men who see the trend of history more clearly than the men of power, always try to persuade the oligarchs to modify their rule and to make it more compatible with the new situation. But the men of power always put off the wise men with minor concessions. The wise men hopefully believe that the minor concessions bear the promise of more generous concessions to the new situation. They are bound to be mistaken in this

33

hope because a given oligarchy cannot make all the concessions which a new situation requires without losing its power. In the contemporary instance the modern industrial oligarchy cannot eliminate unemployment and the threat of international war without sacrificing rights of ownership which are the very basis of its social power. In the final crisis the oligarch therefore defies the wise men and tempts fate. When he finds his reign suffering from a loss of reverence and prestige he attempts to maintain it by sheer power. Thus he increases the injustices and exactions of his rule and multiplies the social resentments which will ultimately prove to be the engines of his undoing.

The wise men who see the logic of history so plainly always live under the illusion that the men of power can finally be persuaded to see what they see. They suffer from this illusion because they do not realize how much the collective life of man moves by impulse rather than by reason. Oligarchies and social systems are actuated by the will-to-survive in narrow and unimaginative terms. They cannot see that the will-to-survive, when it has grown fearful and frantic, is transmuted into a desperate and futile will-to-power and that the will-to-power finally makes survival impossible because it arouses the antagonism of all who suffer from its injustices.

Only rare individuals recognize that the will-to-power is so inextricably interwoven with the will-to-live that the effort to destroy the former actually calls the latter into question. The asceticism which flows from such a recognition remains something of a gesture in even the rarest saints; for it must stop short of suicide. It is therefore futile to expect human societies and social organizations, in whom the impulses of nature always express themselves more primitively than in individuals, to bring these impulses under an adequate rational and moral scrutiny and to avert the deadly vengeance of history upon predatory life. The oligarchies which rule a given society are therefore bound to seek the prolongation of their rule by pure force even though it is certain that the attempt will make their ultimate destruction the more inevitable. That is why the disintegration of a social system and the birth of a new one, are certain to be attended by more struggle and conflict, by more tragedy and pathos than our wise men anticipate. They live under the illusion that life, including collective life, can be made fully rational and moral. They have not yet seen with what stubborn inertia life-as-impulse defies the obvious imperatives of life-as-spirit.

III

THE WISE MEN AND THE MIGHTY MEN

THE WISE MEN AND THE
MIGHTY MEN

T HE wise and learned men, the seers and saints,
the philosophers, social scientists and religious idealists who seek to dissuade the oligarchs
of our era from their suicidal policies, conform to a
very old tradition. Since the dawn of history there
have been men of wisdom and virtue who stood before
the king to speak the truth. The modern wise men
have greater confidence that their advice will be
heeded than their predecessors had. But the court
preachers and the prophets of righteousness of every
age have had something of that confidence when they
were either defying or cajoling the men of power.
Their advice and wisdom seemed to them so logical
and persuasive that they never could understand why
the potentates should not be convicted of evil by their
strictures and turned to the paths of righteousness
by their guidance. The priest or the philosopher
standing before the king is a perpetually recurring
picture in human history. It is symbolic of the contest between the conscience of society and its im-

perial impulses, a contest in which conscience does not frequently gain the victory.

Alexander the Great was tutored in his youth by Aristotle; but the political policies of Alexander reveal little evidence of the influence of Aristotelian political and ethical ideals. Nero had no less a teacher than Seneca, the greatest of stoic philosophers. His extravagant tyrannies indicate that the guide of his youth was forgotten when the power of the imperial office excited his lusts and drugged his conscience.

The advisers of mature monarchs were hardly more successful than the tutors of youthful princes. King Ahab paid the prophet Elisha the tribute of regarding him as his accusing conscience but it was a conscience which he sought to circumvent rather than to heed. John Knox, the Scotch reformer, spoke bravely to Mary, Queen of Scots, but he gained nothing from the interview save a reputation for courage.

Sometimes kings consult the wise man or the good man, the seer or saint, so that they may quiet an uneasy conscience by gaining the consent of a pure one for their dubious designs. Thus Henry VIII sought the consent of the humanist Thomas More, for certain warlike policies upon which he intended to embark. The king succeeded in gaining More's uneasy consent by the device of hiding his real motives behind a pretended zeal for the Christian faith. Priestly counsellors are usually beguiled very easily by the monarch's pretensions of piety. Martin Luther, for instance, gives a very naïve report of the Landgrave of Hesse's pious rectitude. "The Landgrave of Hesse is a very wonderful man. If he would forsake the Gospel he might obtain what he pleased from both pope and emperor; but God hath hitherto preserved him steadfast. He sent for me and for Philip Melanchthon, demanding our advice concerning his intended wars; but we, in the highest manner, dissuaded him from his enterprises; we made best use of our rhetoric and entreated him not to disgrace the Gospel and trouble the peace of the empire by wars. Upon this he was greatly vexed and grew very red, though otherwise he was of upright mind."[1] Luther was more than ordinarily simple in accepting a monarch's adherence to his religious tenets as proof of his virtue. The request of a Henry VIII or a Landgrave of Hesse for advice from non-political counsellors is typical of the strong man's dependence upon the good man and the wise man. The man of power has a conscience but he finds it inconvenient. He tries therefore to satisfy it without obeying it. That is why he uses men of pious reputation in his ritual of self-deception.

There are always priests and philosophers who are too astute to be taken in by the pretensions of the mighty men; and sometimes they are successful in en-

[1] Luther's *Table Talk: Some Fragments* (London, 1832), p. 106.

forcing the claims of conscience against power. Occasionally the strong man yields to the good man of unyielding and disinterested courage. Stephen Langton, an English bishop of great resolution, was able to defy the mighty Pope Innocent III and the surly King John; and Hugh of Avalon, Bishop of Lincoln, successfully matched monastic virtue against royal power.

Usually the man of power does not yield. He beguiles and captivates his more guileless counsellors and dismisses or even destroys his more astute and courageous ones. Frequently he allows himself to be criticized as long as the criticism does not threaten his policy. The youthful Kaiser Wilhelm had a court preacher who preached a paternalistic type of Christian socialism. The Kaiser was intrigued until the ideas of the court preacher, Frederick Stoecker, prompted the formation of a political party, whereupon he was dismissed. Some of our modern critics of the social order take mere criticisms so seriously because they have not yet learned that rulers and men of power are offended by criticism only when it is implemented by political policy. Moral critics are tolerated; but the same toleration is not extended to political foes. Power endows the exercise of self-interest with immunity, at least in the immediate instance, and criticism is therefore harmless. Only when it threatens to arouse political resentments and to create an inimical political power is it a peril to the oligarch and dealt with accordingly. Indeed the mighty man may welcome criticism, if it is not politically implemented, partly because it gives a semblance of morality to the exercise of his power and partly because he is probably more moral and humane as a person than is his rule and moral criticism appeals to his finer sensibilities. An autocrat like Frederick the Great was glad to attach Voltaire, critic of autocracy, to his court and Katherine II of Russia welcomed the French encyclopedist Diderot. They would have been less welcome had they not been foreigners, for in that case their political opinions would have had more political significance.

The recalcitrance and stubbornness of the man of power before the strictures and admonitions of the wise man are not simply due to personal defects or self-deceptions. The real cause lies in the representative character of the oligarch. He expresses not only his own impulses but those of a social group, a class or a nation. He is the incarnation of a *raison d'état*. He may be personally the kindest and most considerate of men, in which case he will do what he can to soften the inevitable injustice of his rule by personal generosities. The annals of history are replete with the kindnesses of noble kings as well as the inhumanities of vexatious ones.

The industrial oligarchy which controls modern

society is no exception to this rule. The philanthropies of the overlords of our era may frequently spring from an honest desire to alleviate human suffering. But the generosities of even the most sensitive do not extend to the point of yielding the sources of their power in the interest of a larger justice. If one of them should actually go to this length, as for instance a Robert Owen, he will be disappointed to discover that his actions are resented by other members of his class. They will regard his actions not only as treason to their interests but as treason to society; for they will inevitably identify the particular social order which they have created with the principle of order itself and will regard the threat of a competing political order as synonymous with the peril of chaos. They will think of themselves as priests, preserving the sanctities of the temple of civilization and they will be only partly conscious of the fact that they are at least as interested in the golden chalices on the temple's altar as in the sanctities which the chalices symbolize.

The fact that a moral judgment upon an outmoded society does not become effective, no matter how justified, until it is executed by an invasion of barbarians whether from within or without (the barbarian executors of judgment upon modern society being the disinherited classes), gives plausibility and even a measure of justification to the moral pretensions of the men of power. The disintegration of any society actually has the threat of a barbarian inter-regnum in it.

For all these reasons the men of power are not as amenable to the counsels of the wise men as the whole school of liberal rationalists assume. There is some-thing rather pathetic about the simple confidence of our social scientists and preachers of international and economic righteousness in the redemptive power of their advice. They are quite sure that nothing but a "cultural lag" prevents modern society from curing its vices. They attribute to disinterested ignorance what ought to be ascribed to interested in-telligence. Even when they recognize the force of self-interest in social policy, they preserve a simple faith in their ability to persuade society to cease from the suicidal policy of pursuing self-interest too nar-rowly. Thus Walter Rathenau preached interna-tional conciliation to a Germany smarting under de-feat. Rathenau was murdered and Hitler has ef-faced the last remnants of Rathenau's influence upon German politics. Sir Arthur Salter prescribed ten necessary steps for the recovery of western economic life. Every one of the prescribed steps requires a sacrifice of national prerogatives and class privileges obviously impossible to achieve.[2] But the liberal

[2]Sir Arthur Salter, *Recovery*. For similar optimistic advice to modern economic and political leaders see also J. M. Keynes, *Essays in Persuasion*.

minds seem not to be dismayed by this fact. They continue to preach righteousness and hope that ultimately their words will soften hard hearts. The burden of their message is that the world needs a more equitable distribution of income and more international accord. But tariffs continue to rise and international economic and disarmament conferences fail. Stuart Chase, H. G. Wells, Norman Angell, and J. M. Keynes and a host of lesser social scientists continue for all that to insist on the necessity of national and international planning, always hoping and assuming that the anarchy of our political and economic life is due to our ignorance and that an effective pedagogy will correct our ills. The modern oligarchs do not behead these wise men. They merely ignore them. The British tories of today even permit a very sentimental preacher of international righteousness to head their cabinet.

The spirit of liberalism, which has provided a welcome lubricant for some of the smaller frictions of society, really produces a form of blindness when it tries to estimate the more inclusive facts and tendencies of human history. Sociologists, whose special business it is to study the realities of social life, seem to be particularly obtuse in dealing with the profounder and more tragic aspects of human history. With no perspective upon human history but the prejudices with which the optimism, the rationalism

and the individualism to the liberal tradition have endowed them, they seek to give these prejudices scientific prestige by clothing them in jargon borrowed
from the more exact sciences. Many of them are still
singing of progress while more realistic souls behold
the tragic spectacle of a civilization slowly destroying itself. Pessimistic doubts and misgivings may
haunt the thoughts of modern historians, but the
sociologists, in America at least, still follow the Spen-
cerian optimism, first elaborated for American socio-
logical thought by Lester F. Ward. Scientific ped-
antry, applied to the complexities of history, where
precise scientific methods screen out little facts and
lose important ones, has served to atrophy nineteenth-
century optimism with particularly pathetic consequences in the social sciences. The scientific pretensions of a science which can never be a science, because
it measures historical and social facts by measuring
rods supplied by the temper of an age, thus merely
serves to preserve that temper against the corrosion
of new facts and situations.

The elaborate scientific pretensions of sociology
are, however, merely incidental to the blindness of liberalism in general. That blindness is derived from
something more than the weakness of the social sciences. It belongs to the superficiality of the whole of
modern culture, which mistook the expansive senti-
mentalities of the eighteenth and nineteenth centuries

47

for a new insight into the nature and meaning of human life. Thus a mood, which was natural to the period when the rising middle classes, with typical short-sightedness, interpreted their victory over the feudal order as the ultimate victory of the human spirit, was made the basis for a new philosophy of history. Naturally a philosophy of history conceived under the influence of the youthful exuberance of an era fails to do justice to the doleful realities of human life, revealed by the premature senility of such an age, facing its doom.

The real basis for all the errors of liberalism is its erroneous estimate of human nature. The wise men of our day cannot gauge the actions of our strong men correctly because they do not understand the tragic facts of human nature. They do not know to what degree the impulses of life are able to defy the canons of reason and the dictates of conscience.

IV

THE SIGNIFICANCE OF FASCISM

THE SIGNIFICANCE OF
FASCISM

PROPHETS of a new social order usually make the mistake of underestimating the vitality of a dying order. Frederick Engels believed in the middle of the nineteenth century that English capitalism would face a revolution in five years. Almost a century has passed since that prediction and it has become apparent that the British social system is, though sick, capable of surviving longer than any national economic system in the western world. The error in these predictions is usually derived from a moral passion which imagines that social injustice will not survive because it ought not to. It does not recognize that history is as lenient as it is inexorable in its processes and is as slow in executing judgment as it is certain to pass a negative judgment upon predatory life. The chief instrument of judgment can be fashioned only by slow degrees. It is created by the resentments of the victims of injustice; and the burden bearers of the world are always inclined more to patience than to heroic rebellion. They are slow to express their resentments and even slower to make them the basis of political policy. Judgments upon social evil are therefore executed only after the evil has cumulated to intolerable proportions. History is thus, like nature, slow to destroy what it has found useless or dangerous and even slower to inter what it has destroyed. For this reason the putrid remains of what was once living and is now dead frequently create a pestilence in society before they are decently buried.

Moribund social systems disintegrate slowly not only because the instruments of their destruction are fashioned so gradually but because they are of tougher fibre than the prophets of a new day realize. They may defy death even long after the diseases of senility have wasted their strength and their foes have given them the mortal wound.

A social system is like a man of robust frame who ignores the disease from which he suffers for months before he finally admits its existence. Even then he prefers to experiment with nostrums rather than submit to the rigorous regimen of a competent physician. Frequently the competent physician is consulted so tardily that the patient defies the doctor's orders in the delirium of fever which frequently precedes death but gives the illusion of a new vitality. The fascist adventures, upon which most of the modern capitalistic nations seem destined to embark before they finally succumb, are most aptly characterized by the metaphor of the delirium which precedes death. They make the death of a moribund social system more inevitable and more painful but they do save it from immediate disintegration by one final show of strength. A dying social system is like some warrior chieftain who becomes more crabbed, tyrannical and brutal as he feels the sceptre of authority slipping from him and seeks to hide his wasted strength by one last effort of desperate courage, inspired by fear and jealousy.

The doctors of a moribund social system, the J. M. Keynes, the Stuart Chases, the Sir Arthur Salters, and the whole host of liberal economists counsel it to substitute a planned economy for anarchy, to eliminate unemployment by raising living standards and to avoid the peril of war by freer international trade. But the imperilled oligarchy of our day, though it may pay lip service to the sweet reasonableness of these counsels, drifts nevertheless toward fascism. The drift is inevitable because it is more natural to hide wasted strength by a desperate venture of power than to arrest its decay by a prudent restraint upon its use.

When the financial and industrial lords of our day find themselves imperilled they therefore seek first of all to consolidate their political power in the state. Hitherto their political rule has been indirect. The modern capitalist has never been an overt political ruler. He has been content to manipulate the processes of political democracy from behind the scenes. But in the hour of crisis democratic principles must be circumscribed. They served very well to defeat the erstwhile feudal foes of capitalism in another age. But they can be appropriated too easily by the new proletarian foes of capitalism to make their continued retention advisable. Democracy gives potential political power to the voter as a mere voter without regard to his status in economic society. Since there are more poor voters than privileged ones it is always possible that the ballot may become an instrument for putting the apparatus of the state in the hands of the disinherited. Indeed the ballot has actually served the purpose of equalizing some of the inequalities of economic society by rigorous taxation policies on the part of political society. Steeply graded inheritance and income taxes have been used to provide social services for the poor.

As long as the old social order does not break down completely the ballots of the poor may be used to circumscribe the rights of economic ownership but they can hardly be used to destroy them. The power of propaganda and the prestige of an established order may be relied upon to persuade the poor to vote contrary to their own ultimate interests. A constitution, whether written or un-

written, which defines the alternatives upon which
votes may be taken is bound to exclude alternatives which aim at the destruction of a given social system. This is inevitably the case, no matter what the claims and pretensions of constitutional
freedom may be, because every constitution is no
more than the rational and legal codification of a
given equilibrium of social power. A completely new
equilibrium cannot therefore be established within
terms of the rational justification of the old one.

When, however, the disintegration of an old order
has reached so obvious a stage that traditional loyalties and credulities are disturbed, and the accepted
presuppositions embodied in the old order are ques-
tioned, democratic principles may actually become a
peril to the old order and they are abrogated by some
subterfuge or other. "The unity of the state," de-
clared the German Vice-Chancellor von Papen in a
recent address, "is achieved from above. The anarchic and divisive forces come from below. Fortu-
nately national-socialism has been able to win the
masses for the ideal of a unified state but we must
not expect such a miracle to occur again. We need
a constitution which protects us against the perils of
chaos residing in the formless masses." Von Papen's
confession is interesting not only for its frank disavowal of the principles of democracy but for its ad-
mission that Hitler's demagogy, a characteristic

fruit of democracy, was a tool for the destruction of democratic principles.

A dying capitalism is under the necessity of abolishing or circumscribing democracy, not only to rob its foes of a weapon, but to save itself from its own anarchy. The competitive freedom of *laissez-faire* capitalism becomes a dangerous hazard in the day of crisis, and it is therefore replaced by state capitalism in which the state both restricts the freedom and supports the weakness of the old property system. Even when the political development is not avowedly fascist the tendency to substitute state capitalism for the old *laissez-faire* economy is obvious, as for instance in England and America.

The basis of fascism's political power is provided by a union of the capitalistic and the military classes, who make use of the confused lower middle classes to augment their strength. In Italy the landed aristocracy participates in, or is at least friendly to, the regime. In Germany it helped fascism come to power but has been excluded from its counsels since. The leader of the landed gentry, Hugenberg, has been dismissed from the government in which the representatives of the petty bourgeoisie, Hitler and Goebbels, have the obvious authority, while Thyssen represents the big industrialists behind the scenes and Schacht holds semi-official power for the financiers in the Reichsbank. The fascist political construction in

Germany is thus more dependent upon the amateur army recruited from the lower middle classes and less upon the older military castes than is the case in Italy, though in both cases private political armies augment the police power of the old state.

The class antagonisms of a disintegrating social order are momentarily resolved in fascism, partly by nationalistic hysteria and partly by the use of force against radical and proletarian groups. Fascism thus combines demagogic skill with military power to maintain internal unity. The demagogy is necessary not only to arouse the whole nation to nationalistic passions but to confuse the lower middle classes and exploit the force of their numbers for the political purposes of the imperilled industrial and financial rulers. In the case of German fascism, Hitler has used the money of the big industrialists, who feared a revolution, in order to recruit a private army from the impoverished middle classes, who were promised a revolution. The failure of proletarian radicalism to come to terms with the middle-class problem, plus the natural political ineptitude of the middle classes, establish the basis for this curious alliance between big industrialists and the discontented masses of the middle class. That such an alliance can hardly become the basis of stable power is already revealed in Germany, where discontented "storm troopers" talk and dream of a "second revolution" and an anxious government discourages such sentiments as bringing discredit on "the revolution."

Fascism aggravates the international problems from which modern civilization suffers and its frantic effort to arrest the disintegration of national unity can only result in making the final dissolution of internal political conflicts more sanguinary than they might otherwise have been. The international problem is aggravated because both the fascist economics of national self-sufficiency and the demagogic exploitation of nationalistic sentiment, for purposes of obscuring the economic motives of fascism, make international peace more difficult, if not quite impossible. It is difficult, for instance, to see how Hitler's Germany can finally avoid war with either France or Poland.

Fascism heals the internal breach within the nation for the moment by the sheer use of force and the manipulation of popular hysteria. But governments cannot maintain themselves by force alone. The power of governments rests upon reverence as much as upon force. Fascist propaganda tries to supply the element of reverence by cultivating a romantic attitude toward "Den Fuehrer" or "Il Duce." But this romanticism is anachronistic. The prestige of traditional monarchs on their throne and the reverential loyalty of their subjects cannot be simply recreated even by the most astute propaganda. The claims of autocrats are preposterous if they do not achieve credibility by the support of an ancient tradition; and the tradition must be imbedded in a culture congenial to it. Modern fascism is trying to resuscitate the old monarchial pageantry but the difference between its efforts and the political liturgies which expressed monarchial pretensions is the difference between cheap theatricality and impressive drama.

Furthermore, in Germany at least and presumably in other advanced industrial nations in which fascism is still to be tried, it must deal with rebellious workers who can neither be won by the monarchial pretensions which may appeal to peasants but not to proletarians, nor be cowed into complete submission by fascist terror. The workers are forced to submit to the dictatorship for the moment; but their disaffection remains a constant threat to the ruling powers and a perpetual temptation to destroy their opposition by increasing political oppression until it reaches absurd and self-defeating proportions.

The net effect of fascism must therefore be to guarantee that the end of capitalism will be bloody rather than peaceful. By destroying the last possibility of resolving the conflicts of modern society in democratic terms it makes a revolutionary end of these conflicts a practical certainty. If the German fascist venture is not resolved in a revolution before the next war it is almost certain to be destroyed in the very war which it is helping to generate; for the internal unity which it has achieved is too artificial to outlast a war. A war will merely put weapons into the hands of the suppressed rebellious multitudes who will welcome the opportunity of turning an international war into a civil conflict. Some of the very groups from which the fascist "storm troops" are now recruited might conceivably make common cause in such a conflict with the radical forces whom they are now suppressing. It is hardly conceivable that the artfully constructed compromise between reactionary and revolutionary sentiment which enables fascism to use discontented middle classes to fight the battles of the capitalists, will outlast the strains and stresses of a war.

It is significant that the capitalists are forced to make their last stand, as did the Roman imperialists, with armies largely recruited from their natural enemies. The "storm troops" of fascism recruited from the lower middle classes are like Roman legions filled with Teutonic soldiers. The security of such military power is not very great in the final crisis. The financial oligarchs, unlike the feudal lords, do not fight their own battles and do not reign in the state in which they rule. They must hire demagogues both to reign in their state and to recruit their armies from the disaffected multitudes who are impoverished by the disintegration of their social system. It would be a rather fitting historical justice if they would be finally defeated through the disloyalty of military forces created by their hired demagogy. Since demagogy is a vice of democracy, they would thus come to an ignominious end through a corruption of the democratic ideals just as they lived and reigned by exploiting and corrupting democratic principles.

V

THE BRIEF GLORY OF THE
BUSINESS MAN

THE BRIEF GLORY OF
THE BUSINESS MAN

THE dominion of the modern industrial and commercial oligarch will be of very brief duration even if it does not perish as quickly as its foes predict and hope. If it should last another century its rise and fall would be compassed by less than three centuries. That is a very brief hour of glory. Compared with the longevity of feudalism, the reign of the business man seems pathetic in its brevity.

The mediæval culture and feudal civilization were some five centuries in developing toward the golden era of the thirteenth century; and another five centuries were required to reduce the imposing structure to complete decay. The decline began in the fourteenth century in which the rise of nominalism, always a quiescent element in mediæval social theory, revealed that the old sense of the organic unity of society was in the process of decadence. Not until the middle of the nineteenth century was the business man able to establish his empire firmly on the domain once ruled by the feudal lord. Through those five centuries the mediæval structure was subjected without succumbing to every conceivable shock known to history. Its papal internationalism, conceived by Hildebrand and firmly established by Innocent III, withstood the rising tide of nationalism for many centuries. Commercial nationalism, Machiavellian politics and the loss of prestige through the Reformation did finally combine to destroy the power and pretensions of the international papacy; but it resisted the corrosion of these new forces for centuries.

The economic organization of the middle ages, dominated by the church on the one hand and the landed gentry on the other, was equally robust in withstanding the vicissitudes of history. The invention of gunpowder robbed the lord in his castle of his prestige as protector of the working community. Rising commerce and industry gave the urban trader and banker superior economic power over the landed aristocrat. The necessities of trade required the unification of nations so that commerce could be conducted with less let and hindrance and therefore gave the king, supported by the trader and banker, a new power over the lord. The Renaissance and Reformation shook the authority of the religious dogmas and cultural presuppositions which gave the feudal organization of society its moral prestige. But all of these forces combined did not destroy feudalism.

The science of the eighteenth century and the industrial revolution of the nineteenth century had to strike their blows before feudalism finally succumbed. In the thought of the eighteenth century a rationalistic idealism supported the democratic aspirations of bourgeois life with "laws of nature," supposedly drawn with scientific accuracy from the phenomena of nature and history. Thus a weapon was found to destroy the prestige of the "laws of God" by which mediæval civilization sanctified its social structure. It is interesting to note in passing that the mythological character of these "laws of nature" was not fully revealed until this new civilization, which the business man built on the ruins of feudalism, began to fall into decay.

The irrational presuppositions of every civilization appear reasonable to it as long as it is vital. The illusions of the "age of reason" were therefore, in a sense, both a proof that old mythologies had lost their vitality and a sign that a new age needed a new faith to destroy the faith of the old. The age of reason either gave feudalism its death blow or fully revealed the senile decay from which it was suffering. Yet feudalism did not pass out completely until the industrial revolution of the nineteenth century dissolved the old social relations in the new mechanisms of finance and industry and made the new accumulations of commercial and industrial wealth too powerful to be resisted.

In spite of all of these defeats neither the mediæval culture nor the feudal civilization and social organization are completely destroyed. The Catholic Church still lives and the old landed aristocrats have maintained a degree of social prestige in many nations. In England the feudal aristocracy learned how to absorb the plutocracy and thus escaped defeat at the latter's hands to this day. The processes of history are lenient as well as inexorable; and wherever an old force yields to rather than resists a new force in history it is usually able to save a remnant of its glory. It is only when, as in Russia, a decaying oligarchy continues its living death far beyond its day and meets new forces with blind desperation, that it is completely destroyed.

It is significant that the business man could not defeat the landed gentry without having the worker press closely upon the heels and using his aid to achieve a triumph over feudalism. There were proletarian rumblings in the bourgeois thunder of the French Revolution. In England the middle classes were unable to secure the franchise without exploiting the threat of the rebellious laborer against the aristocracy. In Germany a bourgeois republic was not established until 1919 and organized labor was more influential in its establishment than the commercial classes themselves. In Russia the middle classes enjoyed only a few months of anxious sovereignty under Kerensky before the revolt of labor overtook them. Only in America, where no feudal traditions prevailed, was the middle class able to establish a thoroughly bourgeois republic without the aid of organized labor.

Against the impressive display of the vitality of a dying feudal culture the brief day of power and glory of the business man's regime is a rather pathetic spectacle, even if it should succeed in prolonging its sickly days for another century.

Why should its day have been so brief? One reason has already been considered. It used more dangerous tools than the older empire. It lived and died by the modern machine. It achieved its power through the machine's productivity and declined because of its overproductivity. The machine, in other words, hastened the process by which social injustice creates the instruments of vengeance against its evils. Furthermore the machine sharpened the instruments of warfare by which social antagonisms have been traditionally resolved. It therefore made every war a peril to the whole fabric of society. Modern technology not only made the instruments of slaughter more destructive but also increased the intensity of cohesion within the fighting nations, so that nations rather than armies were embattled and their martial ardors bankrupted the treasury and enervated the vitality of whole peoples.

Yet this alone would not account for the brevity of the dominion of the commercial overlord. Perhaps an additional reason may be found in the mechanical character of the civilization which he built. The civilization which is passing was a money civilization. That means that the complexities of social relations were controlled by the mechanisms of commercial exchange. The human factor in every social relation was suppressed and obscured. The squires of old were not more just to their serfs than the modern industrialist to his workers. But the injustices of landowners were both mitigated and veiled by the personal relations which obtained between master and serf. So powerful was this sense of *noblesse oblige* on the one side and of loyalty and obedience on the other that it extended even to the monarch upon his throne. The king ruled partly by the power of the armies he was able to support but partly by the personal devotion and obedience given to his person by the common man. This obedience and devotion had in it elements of both reverence for his exalted position and filial piety toward him as the father of his people. It was the proof of the organic character of mediæval life; and it was not easily destroyed even when the monarch or lord completely discredited and outraged this loyalty by his brutalities and extravagances. Its persistence, in spite of disappointments, was not merely the result of the credulity of the hum-

70

ble peasant. It was the product of the more personal, direct and human relations of an agrarian society.

The democracies of the business man supposedly substituted the "consent of the governed" for this reverence for authority as the cement of social cohesion. But this neat theory does not take into account that all democracies turn into oligarchies, that some one always wields the actual power and that power alone cannot maintain itself where reverence is lacking. The common man, even in industrial civilizations, tends to give loyalty and obedience to any power which is able to establish itself and wield authority. But the measure of his devotion is limited. The lords and barons of industry have never been able to count upon it to any considerable degree. Tocqueville foresaw this defect in the new industrial civilization at its very beginning a hundred years ago. He wrote: "The manufacturer asks nothing of the workman but his labor: the worker expects nothing from him but his wages. The one contracts no obligation to protect, nor the other to defend; and they are not permanently connected by either habit or duty. . . . Between the workman and the master there are frequent relations but no real partnership."[1]

The so-called "captains of industry" were for this reason never really captains. They could not count on the loyalty of their men even in the early day of

[1]*Democracy in America,* Part II, Bk. II, Ch. 18.

their vigor. Industrial society had the seed of its destruction, class antagonisms, in it from the very beginning. It is instructive, moreover, that the commercial and industrial oligarchs who have ruled modern society for nearly a hundred years have never dared to rule the state, which served their interests, directly. They have had to use either kings or demagogues to control the state for them. One reason why capitalism is still more firmly entrenched in England than in any modern nation is because the plutocracy was able to exploit the prestige and the political arts of the aristocracy and the monarchy. The remnants of feudalism give the present social order a vitality in England which it lacks in other nations.

Even in America, where the business man completely controls politics, he has never dared to grasp the actual authority of government. The people might envy the success of a captain of industry or finance but they distrusted him too much to empower him with the more obvious sanctions of government. They preferred some obscure lawyer, particularly if he could boast of lowly origins and could thus add a living testimony to the glories of the democratic creed. In Germany a demagogue rules where once the kaiser reigned. Before him a Hindenburg, Junker and army man, rather than any of the lords of modern German industry, was chosen to symbolize the unity of a sadly divided people. A business man would have been impossible for such a position because he would have vivified rather than obscured the social war which divided the nation. The financial and industrial oligarch is an inadequate symbol of national unity and is distrusted as a national leader not simply because his will-to-power has been brutal. He has not been more brutal in intent than other oligarchs. He is merely, together with those who hold him in contempt, the victim of an impersonal and mechanical civilization, which permits the potent forces of collective impulse to express themselves without either the restraint of conscience or a decent veil of social liturgy. The latter is as important as the former. A society maintains its self-respect not only by the effort to restrain the brutality of its collective behavior but by hiding the realities of its social life from itself.

The industrial oligarch of the modern period has cut a very poor figure as a social liturgist. He has not been able to elaborate an effective ritual which every society needs to hide the nakedness of its physical life. His age has been too mechanical and therefore too rationalistic for a proper cultus to develop. He has none of the imaginative gifts by which the knights and lords of another age made romance of their lusts; nor has he been able to hide his class interests successfully behind the common hopes, fears and aspirations which he shared with his people. No songs have been composed to celebrate his valor and no wandering minstrels have edified firesides by chronicles of his daring. He has had a purely utilitarian relation to his society. His one great advantage was that he could exploit the productive achievements of modern technology and encourage the illusion in his society that his skill and sagacity were the authors of modern prosperity. When that illusion is dispelled there are few so poor to do him reverence. The modern oligarch may, as Henry Ford, inspire admiration and envy, but not reverence. No aura envelops his person. If he fails to "deliver the goods" his prestige soon wanes. He is forced to hire demagogues for the purpose of drumming up the armies by which he intends to make his last stand against his foes. A mechanical society, in short, collapses more quickly than an organic one when its day is done. Mere mechanisms of production and communication are not a lasting cement of social cohesion.

VI

THE SOCIAL STRUGGLE IN AMERICA

VI

THE SOCIAL STRUGGLE
IN AMERICA

WHATEVER the future of western civilization and the certainty of the disintegration of its capitalistic system, it is not
likely that American developments will follow the
general pattern without unique and divergent elements of their own. Each nation has its own peculiarities which tend to confuse the general historical
logic; but American peculiarities are of special moment. America is a still youthful nation, organically
related to a moribund western social economy. The reaction of its youthful temper to the diseases of senility which affect all of the western nations produces
very confusing results and makes all prophecies futile. In temper America is still a nation of pioneers.
The effect upon the American mind of a constantly
expanding economy and advancing frontier is still
noticeable though the individualism of the frontiers-
man has given way to a capitalistic collectivism,
standardization and centralization of power, more
consistently developed than anywhere in Europe.
Germany, for instance, has a much higher percentage

of small tradesmen, independent craftsmen and small factories than the United States.

The disintegration of capitalism through overproduction is more obvious in America than in any other nation but it is not yet obvious to the American mind. Even the average American worker persists in believing that a depression is a mysterious visitation of providence for which no one is particularly to blame. If there is a spirit of rebellion among the impoverished farmers and the unemployed workers, it is not informed by a political philosophy which would give it sustained force. The slightest alleviation of the economic pressure upon the farmer and worker would undoubtedly result in a new acquiescence. The spirit of revolt in America is analogous to the sporadic peasant rebellions of the middle ages rather than to the sustained radicalism of the advanced section of the European proletariat.

The real fact is that there is no authentic proletariat in America. That can develop only when a class feels itself closed in by the destiny of history and the antagonism of other classes and gradually realizes that it can gain emancipation only through class solidarity and strategy. In America workers are still, on the whole, individuals who hope under more propitious circumstances to rise into the comparative comfort of the middle classes. Even the new trade-union energy of the present moment grew not out of the labor movement itself but out of the strategic necessities of a liberal administration which needed a stronger labor movement to act as a police force for its state capitalism.

Since the class struggle has not become a fully conscious one in American life it is foolish to speak of the Roosevelt program as "fascism." Fascism represents the class struggle in its final desperate stages. In our nation the facts of the class struggle are just beginning to rise into the consciousness of farmers and workers. There is no genuine fascism where the old order is not challenged by a revolutionary labor movement. In America there is no such movement, except among an insignificant, largely non-citizen, minority of laborers. The Roosevelt program is really analogous to the semi-liberal, semi-radical tendencies of the Europe of 1919-29 rather than to the fascist tendencies of today. It represents the same effort to change *laissez-faire* capitalism into state capitalism as developed in Europe under the pressure of parliamentary socialist parties. The difference is that in America the economic basis for the political pressure upon the state, which brings state pressure upon business, came from the radical farmer rather than the radical worker. In as far as the Roosevelt movement has a clearly defined economic basis it is certainly western agrarianism. The features in the NRA program which are designed to benefit labor are, in a sense, a gratuitous contribution of western agrarian radicalism to a politically impotent and incompetent labor movement.

When it becomes apparent (as it must in the long run) that political control of private capitalism cannot produce sufficient equality of income to eliminate overproduction and unemployment the stage will be set for a sharper delineation of the social struggle in our American life. The vague liberalism of the Roosevelt administration which has achieved a temporary unity in our national life, challenged only by a few reactionaries on the right and radicals on the left, will then disintegrate into a more obvious conservatism and radicalism. Whether the Democratic Party under Roosevelt moves definitely toward the left when the deepening social crisis requires a more unambiguous political program or (what is more likely) tries to hold some of the eastern conservative interests in the same alignment with its western radicalism, it is bound to be challenged by a more outspoken reactionary movement than any present force. The motive for such a reactionary movement will come from the resentments of big business against increased political control and higher taxation burdens and it will justify itself with the insistence that the state control of capitalism has increased the burdens of business without eliminating unemployment. Such a conservative movement, which is bound to come whether in one or in three decades, will have closer similarities to fascism than the present Roosevelt regime. The present regime is roughly analogous to the labor government of Mr. MacDonald; and the conservative reaction to it will have analogies with Mr. MacDonald's tory government. The conviction that these conservative tendencies must ultimately issue in fascism is based upon the assumption that all western social systems must face a crisis in which the issue between capitalism and socialism is definitely joined, each system sharpening its own position in the process of standing in unqualified juxtaposition to the other. Such an assumption rules out the possibility of a gradual transition from capitalism through state capitalism to socialism. The reason such a gradual transition is ruled out is that no ruling oligarchy reveals any inclination to transfer any more power than is absolutely necessary to maintain the functions of its social system; and all of them incline to regret and to disavow the actual transfers they have made when the moment comes in which they are threatened with a complete loss of power. For this reason the reservations which have been placed upon the power of the economic overlords by the Roosevelt administration can no more be regarded as permanent gains in the direction of a socialized state than the analogous gains of the semi-socialistic governments of Europe in the last decade.

There is, in short, nothing in the unique character of American life which can prevent a social struggle, inherent in the nature of modern society, from working itself out to its logical conclusion. But there are unique elements in our life which may postpone the ultimate crisis until the end of the century. An unambiguous and fateful social struggle is not possible if there are not two social groups, each with a high morale and a strong sense of direction. There is no such group on either the conservative or the radical side in America today. There are only conflicting social sentiments, the fears of an imperilled plutocracy and the resentments of a hungry mass of laborers. But neither fears nor resentments are able of themselves to fashion a political policy. The American plutocracy is as bereft of political instincts as business communities have been from the days of Carthage to this day. It is, moreover, unlike the European plutocracy, unable to lean upon or borrow from the more politically minded aristocracy. The fact is that the political instincts of our business oligarchy are so weak that it might succumb completely in a day of crisis if it were confronted by a powerful and politically sagacious labor movement. But that is equally lacking; and decades of experience may be required to fashion it. The social struggle in America is therefore bound to be inconclusive for decades to come. If a very serious social crisis should develop some immediate way out will be found and some obvious palliative will be applied because rigorous cures and striking alternatives to contemporary policies can be initiated only if a powerful and resolute radical movement is ready to insist upon them.

American capitalism is like a once robust man who suffers from premature senility but fails to note his critical situation, partly because he has enough wealth to escape the immediate consequences of his ineffectiveness, partly because the optimistic psychology of a rather recent youthfulness obscures the tragic facts of his present situation and partly because there is no one about strong enough to snatch the vestiges of power from impotent hands.

VII

THE VIRTUES OF A BOURGEOIS
CIVILIZATION

THE VIRTUES OF A
BOURGEOIS CIVILIZATION

WHILE the industrial oligarch is not an impressive figure under the scrutiny of history it must not be assumed that his civilization has been without merit. Nor can the injustices and brutalities of a bourgeois civilization completely obscure certain moral and social gains achieved by it. The decay of a civilization and the judgment of history upon it do not imply a complete lack of virtue. Life is destroyed because of its sins even when a measure of moral virtue has mitigated its vices. The processes of history are too rough to make a precise discrimination between good and evil possible. A civilization which has outlived its usefulness is destroyed in spite of its virtues. That is what makes the realities of history so outrageous to moralists and why they always insist that future history must be more refined than that of the past. It may be possible, no doubt, for a highly intelligent society to amend its flaws without destroying its solid achievements, but it will never be possible to do this as completely as the moralists insist. Human societies are never completely self-conscious or self-transcendent. They therefore persist too resolutely in their vices to be able to save their undoubted achievements from the disaster which must overtake them.

In the eyes of the proletarian foes of a bourgeois civilization, it is the quintessence of all that is evil. In the mythology of communism capitalism is the principle of evil itself, analogous to the devil in the mythology of orthodox Christians. The complexities of history never reveal or justify these over-simplified abstractions; but it must be admitted that they are potent in arousing those passions which are necessary for, or at least inevitable in, the forces of history which destroy the old and construct the new. If a higher degree of objectivity should provide more discriminating judgments there is always the possibility that they will lame the nerve of action. But there is no reason why the intelligent observer should not attempt an impartial appraisal of the limitations and achievements of an era even if he knows that the rough processes of history will not follow his nice discriminations.

The most outstanding achievement of a bourgeois civilization is its discovery and affirmation of the rights of the individual. The emergence of the individual from the mass has been slowly proceeding since primitive law and custom first recognized individual responsibility in the treatment of crime and conceded the individual minimum rights (at least the right to live) without regard to social function. In a sense the past 200 years have simply brought certain tendencies toward individualism, manifest throughout history, to a logical conclusion. Universal suffrage is the recognition of each individual's right to participate in the organization and direction of society. The fact that the exercise of the franchise does not affect a given equilibrium of social and economic power in society as much as democratic idealists anticipated does not invalidate this democratic recognition of the rights of each individual as a real achievement.

The emancipation of women, historically related to the struggle for a universal franchise, is another achievement of bourgeois individualism. The subjection of women in all previous civilizations was justified by a too consistent derivation of rights from social function. Women had rights only as wives and mothers and not as human beings *per se*. The fact that their social function should have been regarded as inferior to that of the male population may have been due to the primitive glorification of war, it may have been a rationalization of the superior physical strength of the male or it may have been derived from forces inherent in the psychology of sex. At any rate the democratic idealism of a bourgeois civilization granted women inherent human rights which pre-

89

vious civilizations had denied her; and the necessities
of industry gave her the economic power and inde-
pendence to enforce the claims which reason allowed.
There are, of course, perils in modern feminism; for
it tends to deny the organic character of family life
and to give precedence to individuals over the necessities of life's organic relationships. That is the peril
in which every achievement of individualism stands.
Yet it remains a social achievement, having a universal validity beyond the peculiar circumstances of the
bourgeois life which created it.

The humanitarianism of the past 200 years stands
in strange contrast to the inhumanities of industrialism but it is nevertheless a legitimate child of the
modern world. The aged and infirm, the subnormal
and the sick have all been given a consideration by
modern society, unprecedented in human history. In
the mediæval world the church enjoined charity but
society as such assumed little responsibility for those
who had fallen by the wayside. In the modern world
society and the state have accepted as a responsibility
what was regarded as an act of grace in feudal society. The conscious humanitarianism of an industrial
civilization has only mitigated and not abolished the
inhumanities which are partly inherent in the realities of a mechanical society and partly the consequence of the heedlessness of the industrial oligarchs
who control the society. An industrial civilization is

consciously more greedy and less brutal than an agrarian world. Its unconscious brutalities are so enormous that they warn against any sentimental overestimate of the moral significance of its philanthropies. Yet there is solid moral achievement in its humanitarianism.

Perhaps the bourgeois soul is more ready to grant certain inherent rights to each individual (at least in theory) because it has itself a more completely independent and discrete individuality than any previous personality. This is both its virtue and its vice. Rationally this individualism was elaborated by the philosophers of the French enlightenment and by English liberalism from Locke to Bentham. But reason can only work on presuppositions supplied by the temper of an era. The real root of bourgeois individualism is the character of urban life. The man of the city may be mechanically more dependent upon his society than the peasant. But he is not in such intimate organic relation to it. He therefore feels himself to be more completely an individual. His habits and actions are not controlled as closely as is the case in more intimate societies. Furthermore the complexity of urban life and the multiplicity of his social contacts and relationships tend to diminish the hold which any particular social group has upon him. He achieves his freedom partly through the contest for his fealty of various social groups.

Culturally and spiritually urban individualism makes a permanent contribution to the history of the race, whatever its limitations may be. No highly developed personality, or for that matter any personality, can ever be grasped in its uniqueness through the social patterns which form it and the social milieu in which it expresses itself. There are depths of consciousness in each individual self-consciousness which can never be completely exhausted in any social expression. High religion, which is, in one of its aspects, an effort of the "I" to lose itself in, and identify itself with society, is also a profound expression of the soul's rebellion against society. In all great religion the individual finally faces the eternal mystery of life alone; and the very heart of that mystery is the reality of self-consciousness, seemingly dwarfed and yet not dwarfed by a world of physical immensity. Spengler may be right in suggesting that this high degree of self-consciousness is the peculiar characteristic of the Faustian soul, of western man.[1] If so, modern civilization has given it its final development. In this sense a bourgeois civilization has not been wrong in regarding itself as Christian, even if it violated the ethical precepts of Christianity. Christianity's insistence that each soul is of transcendent worth has been partially fulfilled (though secularized in its fulfillment), in the liberalism of modern

[1] Oswald Spengler, *The Decline of the West.*

culture. In no society in which religious experience has illumined the profound depths of individual self-consciousness can society absolutize itself against the individual as completely as communistic society does.

Naturally the individualism of bourgeois liberalism is not a clear gain or a pure virtue. Partly because it is the product of a mechanical civilization and partly because it is the fruit of rationalism, modern individualism is too mechanistic in its conception of society. The organic character of the individual's relation to society can be comprehended and illumined by an adequate mythology but hardly by rationalism; for reason mechanizes human relations. No human society has ever existed in which discrete individuals consciously formed a social group after the manner conceived in the social theory of John Locke and the two centuries of liberalism which have followed his philosophy. In as far as modern society has actually been so inorganic as to approximate the liberal theory it has been without an adequate sense of social responsibility. The unpolitical, desocialized creature who lives in a modern urban apartment house, in a dwelling full of people but without any neighbors, subsisting upon the proceeds of the labor of others with whom he has not the slightest human contacts, is the pathetic product and spiritual victim of a decadent individualistic culture and civilization.

There are indications that communism will substitute a mechanistic collectivism for the mechanistic individualism of a bourgeois civilization. Its collectivism is mechanistic partly because it is, like capitalism, the product of a mechanical civilization and partly because it is, like liberalism, a fruit of rationalism. In this, as in some other respects, communism is too much the child of capitalism and lives too much by a precise negation of the vices of the latter to bring real peace and happiness to mankind. One of the pathetic aspects of human history is that the instruments of judgment which it uses to destroy particular vices must belong to the same category of the vice to be able to destroy it. Thus some evil, which is to be destroyed, is always transferred to the instrument of its destruction and thereby perpetuated.

The most dangerous aspect of bourgeois individualism must still be mentioned. It is the ease with which the oligarchs of industrialism are able to exploit libertarian idealism for the purpose of sanctifying their power and their freedom from social control. From the very beginning libertarianism was a tool of the middle classes in their struggle to remove the restraints upon business which a feudal society had maintained in the interest of the landed gentry. The virtue of *laissez-faire* economics was that it destroyed the mercantilism by which the feudal nobility derived special privileges from government. Gradually the political economy of classical liberalism, conceived as a tool of the rising middle classes in their struggle with the nobility, became an instrument of the more favored portion of the middle classes, the commercial and industrial overlords. The dogma, which emancipated their fathers from subjection to the nobility, became in their hands a justification of socially unrestrained commercial and industrial greed. Their fathers honestly believed that competition would provide a sufficient check upon the self-interest of trader and manufacturer. But they built an economic system in which economic power became too monopolistic to be subject to any automatic checks. Yet they persisted in the individualistic creed of the fathers and thereby prevented society from checking their greed in the interest of consumer and worker.

This modern corruption of the creed of individualism has naturally resulted in a cynical reaction toward its idealistic pretensions. The worker, in his cynicism toward the hypocrisy of this individualism, will naturally tend to discredit the solid achievements of middle-class individualism to a degree not warranted by the facts of history.

VIII

THE INDIVIDUAL AND
INDIVIDUALISM

VIII

THE INDIVIDUAL AND INDIVIDUALISM

THE creed of individualism may lead to the enslavement of individuals by powerful men and groups because it discourages adequate social checks upon their power. It may also lead to the absorption of the individual into the crowd by robbing individuality of the resources necessary to resist the mass. The tendency of individualism to destroy the inner resources of the individual is a sad and pathetic aspect of modern history.

The individual draws the sustenance of his self-conscious individuality from his organic relation to his social group, his family, his craft and his community. While he has always been in the peril of being too completely absorbed in these primary social groups and while his essential liberties have been frequently too rigorously curtailed by them he has also achieved the highest degree of individual self-respect in these intimate relations in which personality is revered, respected, trusted and relied upon. A mechanical civilization weakens these organic relations and thereby destroys robust individuality. The completely modern man has no social relations sufficiently organic to give his life real significance. The modern urban man, shuttling between his office and his apartment, is hardly as significant a person as a traditional peasant in his village community. In his office or factory he is a unit in a vast mechanical enterprise; and the domain into which he retreats for his hours of rest and leisure has been reduced to a little apartment, barely large enough to serve his minimum physical needs. His family is significantly a small one, children having become a liability in the urban world. This little group of wife and, probably, one child is the only social group to which his life is really organic.

The influence of urban life upon this primary social cell, the family, is not restricted to the diminution of its size and its living quarters. The family has lost its organic contact with the larger family as well. The whole web of secondary blood ties, of the multiple relationships which are cast about every individual in village life and enlarge every family into a kind of clan, has been destroyed in highly developed urban life. Married brothers do not feel themselves responsible for each other or for each other's children as they do in the peasant villages from which their fathers sprang. The disintegration of the larger family under the influence of urban life is one of the elements which make for the spiritual poverty of modern urbanites. The fact that the size of the individual family is usually reduced under urban conditions and that no common economic or social enterprise, shared by parents and children, helps to cement the family tie, further adds to the attenuation of organic relations in city life.

A mechanical civilization and a rationalistic culture not only reduce the size and significance of the family but they affect the very core of the family, the relation between husband and wife. What is regarded as a sacrament in the traditional world is reduced to a social contract in the bourgeois liberal world. The binding force of the union is conceived partly in romantic and partly in rational terms. It is romantic in conception in as far as the love of two individuals for each other, without regard for the family interests which plan and which are united in the more traditional marriage of the feudal period, is regarded as the only legitimate basis of marital union. It is rational and liberal in conception in as far as the union, initiated by the love of two discrete and atomic individuals for each other, is sealed by a legal contract, analogous to the rationalized social actions of the political and economic world. It is typical for the temper of modernity that such contracts are frequently negotiated with many misgivings about the loss of freedom involved in them and legal provisions are therefore made for the recapture of freedom should the relationship prove intolerable.

It would be ridiculous to maintain that the traditional family could exist under modern conditions without resulting in unnecessary sacrifices of individual freedom or that the modern family does not possess some spiritual advantages over the past. But all this does not change the fact that the history of the modern family is symbolic of the whole history of modern society in which the individual gains a Pyrrhic victory. He becomes completely the individual, so completely that he lacks the resources to maintain himself against the crowd, into which he is submerged. He is like a cut flower, which sports its fragrance for a moment without competing with the riot of fragrance and color in the garden; but it is soon withered.

The rationalistic character of communist culture is attested by the fact that it seeks consciously to reduce the family to even less significance than bourgeois culture has unconsciously done. It furthermore excludes the romantic element (as a bourgeois accretion) so that the family becomes a highly rationalized and "efficient" institution for the procreation of the race. This is done for the very purpose of fitting the individual more completely into the mass. Here is one of several instances in which communism reveals itself to be the victim and not the nemesis of a capitalistic civilization, destined not to correct the weaknesses of a bourgeois culture but to develop them to the last impossible and absurd consistency.

The bourgeois world and the technical civilization play the same trick upon the individual in regard to his craft and vocation as in regard to his family. The individual of a non-technical age was always a type. His manner, costume and physiognomy betrayed him as a peasant, a cobbler, a merchant, a craftsman or a priest. The modern world knows no such typical distinctions. It standardizes not only the dress but also the physiognomy of the man in the crowd (one need only to study the vacuous faces of a typical subway group). The gain is that class distinctions have vanished. (A stenographer cannot be distinguished from an heiress on a New York street, provided one is not an expert in the price of furs.) There are real advantages in this potential equalitarianism of standardization. But no genuine equality has been achieved and character has been lost. The individual ceases to be a type. In the case of those who are very resourceful this means the development of a fuller individuality. For the average individual it means a completer absorption in the mass. Emancipated of the moulding forces of traditional craft and vocation he is not moulded at all. Perhaps this is most obvious in the case of the old handicraftsman who has lost his skill to the machine and has become a mere tender of the automatic machine. He can be as easily replaced as a broken part of the machine.

The loss of individuality of modern urban man is expressed by his dependence upon the crowd. He feels at home only in the mass. He seeks out the crowds which gather at athletic games and public spectacles with almost morbid eagerness. He becomes a unit in the crowd which is harangued by the political demagogue and supplies the political force by which reactionaries and radicals fight the political battles of the modern day. If he desires escape from the workaday world he must find it in the standardized cinema and commercialized amusements. As modern civilization disintegrates and involves itself in national and civil wars he is called upon to become a unit in a great mechanical slaughtering enterprise. So modern civilization creates and destroys the individual.

IX

CHRISTIAN AND BOURGEOIS
INDIVIDUALISM

CHRISTIAN AND BOURGEOIS
INDIVIDUALISM

THE relation of liberal individualism to the individualism of Christianity deserves a further thought. The similarity between them has a double reference. They are both derived from the moral and spiritual insights of the sensitive individual conscience; and they both make the individual an object of special moral concern. In both life is viewed from the vantage point of the conscience of the individual, from which the brutalities and injustices of man's collective life are felt to be a sin and an affront to the human spirit. In one case conscience is sharpened by profound religious insights, and in the other by disciplined intellectual discernments. But in both cases the contest of power, to which a realistic analysis reduces every political relationship, is condemned not only because it represents an irrational and immoral anarchy of life but because the individual is too completely sacrificed to the group by the necessities of the conflict. In each therefore the transcendent or the unique value of individual life is emphasized.

The individualistic tendencies in the Christian religion are obvious on every hand. Jesus believed that there would be joy in heaven over the one sinner who repented and that article of faith signifies the unvarying assumption in the entire history of Christian thought that God is interested and concerned in the destiny and the salvation of the individual soul. Benjamin Kidd rightly attributes to Christianity the primary cause of the achievement of western civilization in freeing the individual from the tyranny of the political group and giving his life a centre of reference by virtue of which he is able to defy the dictates of governments and the efforts of nations to make him a mere tool of their purposes.[1] Even after Christianity was forced to come to terms with the necessities of the political order in which no individual can be completely free or can be regarded as absolutely an end in himself, it always maintained some emphasis in its doctrine which did justice to the unique value of the individual, and to the significance of the ideals projected by the conscience of the individual.

In the main body of Christian orthodoxy the pessimism in regard to the political order was too thoroughgoing to allow for a strong insistence upon individual rights. It was recognized that whatever the moral and spiritual ideal might be, in a "world of sin" individuals would always be claimed by societies and

[1]In Benjamin Kidd, *Principles of Western Civilization.*

nations for the attainment of their own ends, and would sacrifice both their liberty and their equality to the necessities of the communal order. But in the sight of God individuals were to be regarded as still free and equal. The basic assumptions of an individualistic morality were, in other words, transmuted from socio-moral principles to religio-moral ideals. Naturally this solution of the problem easily led the church into premature compromises with the injustices and inequalities of society, but it was in many respects superior to modern liberalism in its recognition of the actual realities of life; for the latter still gives itself to the simple faith that both the ideals and the needs of individuals can be fully realized in an ideal society. It does not see that there is no conceivable society which will ever completely incarnate the highest moral ideals of a sensitive individual or which will fully grant the individual all that his moral nature demands. In pure morality society ought to recognize the individual as an end in himself, and ought to leave him free to find his life by losing it for social ends which appeal to his conscience. In actual history national and other communities will always coerce individuals to serve their purposes whether they will or no. They will try to reduce the unique individual to purely functional significance and they will partially succeed.

The stubborn individualism inherent in the Chris-

tian gospel is revealed not only by the recognition of
the orthodox church that the coercion and the injustice of the actual political order belong to a world
of sin but by the resistance offered by perennial mi-
norities in the church to the compromises with the political order, prompted by this recognition. The ascetics of the mediæval period and the sectaries of the
Protestant church both have their chief significance in
their effort to establish a purer ethic than the necessities of the political order permitted. In the case of
the ascetics political responsibility was explicitly disavowed in order to construct an ideal miniature society in which the law of love, the principles of equality and the ideal of the transcendent worth of the individual would prevail. The fact that the ascetics
separated themselves from ordinary society and from
the responsibilities of family life and property relations proves that they shared some of the pessimism
of the church. They did not believe that a pure moral
ideal could be established in the ordinary political
order. Their "liberalism" was oriented by a more
pessimistic realism than modern rational liberalism
can understand. They expressed that realism not
only by disassociating themselves from the collective
life of man, in which collective impulse so clearly reveals the elements of "nature" in human life; but by
a morbidly rigorous self-discipline which proved that
they understood how the immoralities of society have

110

their origin in the egoism of individuals. One need not follow the ascetics in their monasticism to appreciate the realism which prompted it.

It is significant that in asceticism of the type of Saint Francis' in which the monastic strategy is adhered to less rigorously, the pessimism of orthodoxy is qualified by an optimistic view of human nature which establishes points of reference between Saint Francis and Rousseau. The estimate of the goodness of human nature is not as simple as that of Rousseau and it is therefore accompanied by a rigorous self-discipline. In his paradoxical attitude toward man as a sinner and as a child of God Francis comes very near to the view of Jesus as found in the Gospels, a view which is less simple but more profound than either the pure optimism of modern liberalism or the pessimism of orthodoxy.

The more rigorous sects of Protestantism, the Anabaptists, Mennonites, Quakers and others represent the Protestant corollary to the ascetic movement. Here too an ethic is demanded for society which springs from the insights of the individual conscience, an ethic of love, equality and liberty. Here also the ethic is first of all realized in the intimate religious community, and this is accomplished at the price of sacrificing social responsibility. The asceticism of the sectaries is not as rigorous as that of the monastics. It does not preclude the responsibilities of family life. It enjoins simplicity rather than poverty. It remains within the world more than monasticism. But it refuses to be involved in the coercion and the inequalities of the political and economic order, and it is to that extent ascetic. The sectaries did not as a rule expect their absolute ethic to be progressively realized in history. They were apocalyptic in their interpretation of history, and believed that the Kingdom of God would be established by the grace of God and not by the growing goodness of men. This apocalypticism was the mark of their religious pessimism. In the case of the Mennonites it is unqualified. The Quakers, particularly under modern liberal influence, have a greater admixture of the rational liberal hope for the progressive establishment of an ideal social order through the gradual infiltration of pure moral ideals into the world of politics.

On the whole rigorous moral idealists in the Christian tradition are to be distinguished from modern liberals by the element of moral pessimism in their thought. They did not believe that the highest ideal which the individual could conceive would be either easily or fully established in history. They were too conscious of the sinfulness of human nature for such a faith. They had in other words a profound understanding of the anarchic forces which express themselves in human life, particularly in collective human behavior. This is an unvarying mark of a religious interpretation of human nature.

Modern liberalism distinguishes itself sharply from Christian individualism therefore by its unqualified optimism. It believes with Rousseau in the goodness of natural man; or with Adam Smith in the harmlessness of egoistic man; or with J. S. Mill and the utilitarians in the virtue of prudently selfish men. It believes either that there is an immediate and mystical union between the will of the individual and the general will; or that an automatic social harmony results from a conflict of individual wills; or that reason may easily rob egoism of its anti-social force and establish an identity between self-interest and social interest. In any case, an optimistic view of human nature leads to an optimistic interpretation of human history in which the inertia of natural impulses to moral ideals, particularly in man's collective life, is obscured.

The source of liberalism's superficialities is to be found both in its rationalism and in the mechanism of modern bourgeois society. Rationalism divorces reason from impulse too completely and underestimates the tendency of impulse to defy and corrupt the dictates of reason. The mechanism of modern society abets rationalism in obscuring the power of natural impulse in the collective life of man.

An adequate view of human nature, which does justice to both the heights and depths of human life, and which sees the moral ideal in purest terms and judges historic realities in the light of that ideal is possible only to religion. For the individual never comes to full self-consciousness, and therefore to a consciousness of what is nature and what is spirit in him, until he strains after the absolute and the unconditioned. This yearning after the absolute is the very core of religion. In it he recognizes the infinite possibilities of order and beauty in existence. If the yearning expresses itself in completely consistent terms religion swallows morality and the absolute is defined in terms which empty it of all meaning.

In ethical religion the absolute is defined in moral terms, in the ideal of love, for instance. It becomes the moral obligation to affirm all life rather than the life of the ego, and to subject the self to the demands of life *per se*. In straining after the highest moral possibilities of life the individual becomes the more conscious of the inertia of nature which prevents him from realizing them. He recognizes that there is "law in my members which wars against the law that is in my mind." That is how the consciousness of God and the consciousness of sin become a part of the same religious experience and are inextricably intertwined with each other. The superhuman and the subhuman are touched in one moment of consciousness.

In the more purely rational experience the moral

114

possibilities which are envisaged are not so high and the depths of life are therefore left unillumined. The typical rational morality obscures the conflict between the ethical impulse and egoism by a demand for prudent selfishness involving an ideal of mutuality. The white light of a pure ideal does not illumine the human scene, and the shadows of nature and the dark and cavernous depths of human evil therefore remain undiscovered.

This is the reason why only a religious individualism can be maintained without illusions. A secular individualism is possible only when the individual feels himself emancipated from his organic relations to society and indulges in the vain hope that the insights of a pure conscience may be realized without serious social hindrance. Religious individualism recognizes the roots of society's evils in the self, but it also knows that the impulse toward the ideal is a vital factor in life. Being certain of the spirit it is not afraid to look upon the face of nature. Confident of the reality of the principle of love, and certain in its faith in God it is able contritely to recognize the reality of malignant power in the self and in the world.

The optimism of rational individualism and liberalism is more superficial. It proceeds from individuals who have little sense of the organic relation of the individual to the social whole. It is therefore the characteristic attitude of the bourgeois soul, liv-

ing in mechanical urban civilizations. Its lack of organic relation to society leaves it without a profound
understanding of the inertia of nature which is most
clearly revealed in collective human behavior; and
its lack of religious profundity robs it of an understanding of this inertia within the soul of the individual. It is therefore able to assume that the moral
possibilities which the reason of an individual is able
to envisage are immediately capable of realization in
history, provided only that a little more education
purify the reason of others to the degree of purity
it feels itself to have attained. Thus the atomic individual in a mechanical civilization is an optimist at
the very moment when his society moves and is moved
by the impulses of nature, toward the doom of self-
annihilation.

Only a religious individual can lift himself above
society without illusion and without despair. For by
straining after those final possibilities of life which
transcend the human a morality can be achieved which
surpasses the mediocre realities of social life; and
only by recognizing the reality of evil in the same moment in which the possibility of the good is realized,
can individual morality express itself without becoming involved in unwarranted pride as it seeks escape
from despair and disillusion.

The real affinity between religious and rational liberalism is perfectly illustrated by the manner in

116

which desperate liberals hope that Gandhi will justify their faith in the possibility of a victory of the spirit over nature in the world of politics. Everywhere in the western world their hopes that reason and spirit will conquer impulse and reduce the anarchies of politics to harmony are being disappointed. But in the Orient there seems still to exist a slight possibility of victory. There "soul force" may yet conquer the power of an empire.

There is a slightly pathetic aspect in this transference of liberal hopes to Gandhi's frail person. After all his liberalism is religiously and not rationally oriented. While there are touches of romanticism in it, he is more conscious of the power of evil in the world than the rational liberals, and he knows that devils cannot be cast out except by much fasting and prayer. He does not count on any easy victory of the spirit. Furthermore it must be considered that the tropical climate of India, the meagre sustenance of its soil for its millions and the ages of discipline in religious otherworldiness have reduced the physical power of the Indian and mitigated the force of his will-to-live on the level of natural life. The white man is a fiercer beast of prey than the Oriental, particularly the Indian. His lusts are therefore not tamed as easily by the spirit as the Indian's. Gandhi's strategy may therefore not avail in the western world, even as it is not certain that it will avail with the physically

117

more robust Moslems of India nor with the more intransigeant British imperialists.

Gandhi will extend the power of the spirit over the world of nature in collective life as far as it can be extended at any time in this century. He will succeed therefore as he has already succeeded, even though the success may be only a qualified one in the final analysis. His fast for the sake of abolishing untouchability suggests that he will end his days as a religious saint rather than a political leader. Indian politics will not be without marks of his influence. But ultimately the Indian will must be implemented by something more than Gandhi's technique if it is to conquer the British will, symbolized by men like Winston Churchill. The cynical and realistic Churchill, with his unyielding imperial ambition, is the perfect symbol of the inertia of nature in politics. The spirit can always gain a moral victory over such a figure simply by subjecting it to moral condemnation. But a political victory is possible only on the political level. Liberalism is reluctant to admit this fact; yet all history attests its truth. A political victory is won by political means. It is therefore never a clear moral victory, though there may be moral possibilities within it.

X

MYTHOLOGY AND HISTORY.

X

MYTHOLOGY AND HISTORY

I T will be hundreds of years before full justice can
be done to the impressive drama of contemporary history. Only through the perspective of
the centuries can all the complex and multifarious
tendencies and movements of these decades be brought
into a synthetic whole. The comprehension of the
total situation will require the co-operation of many
minds as well as of many generations. The political
economists will be able to chart the self-destruction
of capitalism in terms which will make it seem that it
is an experiment in physics rather than a human
drama which we are enacting. Romanticists will see
the figures of great personalities, revolutionary leaders, desperate defenders of the *status quo*, shrewd
compromises between opposing forces, Lenins, Mus-
solinis, Hitlers, and potent personalities yet un-
born; and they will interpret the course of events in
terms of the strength and the weakness of this leader
and that hero. Moralists will find significance in the
fact that injustice destroys itself and that history,
for all its seeming aimlessness, seems to work in the
direction of casting the mighty from their seats and

121

exalting them of low degree. Pessimists will see the lowly exalted to become the new order of the mighty and will wonder whether there is progressive movement in history or only endless cycles of promising victories and new defeats. Artists and dramatists will see both in the whole and in particular parts of this moving course of events the recurring beauty of tragedy in human history; perhaps they will catch a new vision of the significance of the human spirit in its contest with the impulses of nature, in its defeats and in the possibilities of victory through its defeats.

A philosophy of history adequate to bring all of the various perspectives, from those of economists and political strategists to the insights of artists and moralists, into a total unity must be endowed with the highest imagination. It must combine the exact data of the scientist with the vision of the artist and must add religious depth to philosophical generalizations. An adequate philosophy of history must, in short, be a mythology rather than a philosophy. It is precisely because modern culture is too empirically rationalistic that it cannot do justice to the very history of which it is a contemporary spectator. It lacks a vision of the whole which would give meaning to the specific events it seeks to comprehend. A vision of the whole is possible only if it is assumed that human history has meaning; and modern empiricism is afraid of that assumption. Meaning can be attributed to history only by a mythology.

The modern empiricist does not escape mythological interpretations of history in his effort to avoid them. He merely insures their inadequacy by leaving their presuppositions unexamined. Usually he translates the mood of optimism which has characterized the spirit of the bourgeois world into a mythology of progress. In this mythology human history is portrayed as the gradual triumph of mind over impulse. The limitations of middle-class life rather than the actual facts of history determine the outlines of this history-picture. The historical progress toward an ethical goal is portrayed as a gradual cumulation of individual triumphs of reason over nature until the whole of nature is subdued. There is no recognition in such a picture of history of the possibility of catastrophe. Nor is the perspective high enough to discern the possibility of a new and more perfect order in momentary chaos. That is why modern liberalism and empiricism try frantically to save a decaying civilization from complete disintegration and place their pathetic trust in world economic and disarmament conferences, in the hope that they will arrest the process of decay and justify the badly shaken confidence in the inevitability of progress. The culture of modernity is too rationalistic to realize that historical advance may be achieved not so much by a pure triumph of spirit over nature but through a conflict between an old and a new civilization in which forces of nature are arraigned against each other, the force of hungry men, for instance, against the will-to-power of mighty men. Modern culture is too individualistic to comprehend history in terms of a combat between two social organisms, the new organism emerging from the womb of a dying one.

An adequate mythology of history must be able to do justice to the suggestions of meaning in momentary chaos. It must be able to realize that forces which are not immediately conscious of purpose, at least not of ultimate purpose, may be used to weave meaning into the strands of history. It must not be assumed that any mythology of history can do justice to all of its detailed facts nor that it will be absolutely true in the sense that it is the only possible interpretation of all the facts. But neither can it be assumed that a science of history which disavows mythology is more accurate in its description of the detailed facts.

Saint Augustine could regard the disintegration of the Roman Empire with equanimity because he had a mythology, derived partly from the Christian Gospels and partly from Platonism, which enabled him to see the rise of the Catholic Church as more than an adequate compensation for the disintegration of the empire. His mythology actually validated itself within limits because it created a church which became a residuary legatee and receiver in bankruptcy of a bankrupt empire Interpretations of history actually tend to verify themselves, when rigorously held, because they direct the course of history toward an imagined inevitable goal. Something of the Augustinian conception has remained with Christian orthodoxy, both Catholic and Protestant. It was essentially an individualistic mythology because it permitted the sensitive spirit to transcend the vicissitudes of history, even to consign them to a realm of comparatively meaningless cycles and recurrences, and to find peace either in an institution of grace (the Catholic doctrine) or in a personal experience of grace (the Protestant version) in which a realm of meaning above history was discovered.

It is significant that the Christian sects of the disinherited, who were too immersed in the social situation to allow themselves this kind of religious escape from history, expressed their hope in apocalyptic terms and saw the whole of history redeemed. In this they merely returned to the more Jewish conception of history, against the conceptions introduced into Christianity by Greek individualism and rationalism. With the prophets, with Jesus and with the early church they longed for the day when the whole of history would be redeemed by a triumph of spirit over impulse and nature. In this sense the apocalypticism

of the sects and of early Christianity had some similarity with the faith of modern liberalism in the redemption of historic society. It differed from liberalism in the important particular that it did not expect man to accomplish this triumph by his own resources. It was too conscious of man as a source of
evil and too imbued with the idea of sin to trust in a
man-made ideal society. Such a society would be established by the grace of God.

It is very easy for modern man, with his strong
sense of self-sufficiency and potential power, to sneer
at this type of apocalypticism and to call attention
to the peril of moral lassitude which inheres in it. The
pathetic hopes of contemporary millenarian sects
would seem to justify such strictures. But the modern man does not realize that these apocalyptic hopes
had at least the merit of recognizing that history is
something more than what individual rationalists and
idealists want it to be and that the vast forces of history do not respond as easily to our ideals as the
modern individualist imagines. If the good is to be
established in history that must be done at least partly
by evil destroying itself and not by making evil people good through a little more education.

The Marxian mythology stands between the
mythology of Christian sects and the faith of liberalism. With liberalism it emphasizes the faith in
human responsibility for the historic process. (The

ablest exponent of dialectic materialism in America, Sidney Hook, is a former disciple of John Dewey and properly insists that the dialectic process between human consciousness and the "objective historical conditions" is not unlike Dewey's interpretation of the function of mind in directing historical growth.) With the Christian sects, the Marxian realizes that historical patterns are developed not merely by those who consciously try to weave them. It knows, in other words, that history may be interpreted in terms of meaning even when the forces of history are not conscious of the end which they are achieving. Thus Marxism believes that capitalism is destroying itself by its own inherent "contradictions" and that it is fashioning the instruments of its own destruction.

Marxism is certain that this interpretation of contemporary history is scientific rather than mythological. It has actual historical data to prove that the increased concentration of capitalistic power makes it more vulnerable and invites its destruction; and that the increased misery of the multitudes generates the revolutionary zeal by which the old order will be destroyed. However much such a thesis may claim scientific validity, it is clearly a mythological construction. Events in history are read from a perspective achieved by an ethical and even a religious passion. A force in history is assumed which makes for the triumph of man's highest social ideals, interpreted by the Marxian as that of equal justice. The Marxian does not share the liberal hope that an ethical ideal is easily achieved in history, nor yet the classical religious belief that only God himself can redeem the chaos of history and reduce it to harmony. The Marxian hope is rather that processes in history support those who are willing to affirm these processes.

How much of a mythology the Marxian "science" of history really is, is inadvertently revealed by Marx himself in the words "History would have a very mystical character if 'accidents' had played no part. These accidents enter of course by themselves as component parts in the general process of development, being outweighed by other accidents. But the acceleration and retardation depend to a considerable degree upon these accidents among which figure the character of people who stand at the head of the movement." If the recognition of accidents which may retard or accelerate but not change the general direction of history is the only element in Marxian philosophy of history which saves it from being "mystical" it must be admitted that the mystical content is still fairly high.

Trotsky frankly avows this faith in an inexorable tendency in history. In the concluding paragraph of his autobiography *My Life* he writes: "On April 26, 1852, Proudhon wrote to a friend in prison: 'The movement is no doubt irregular and crooked but the tendency is constant. What every government does in turn in favor of revolution is inviolable. What is done against it passes over like a cloud. I enjoy watching this spectacle in which I understand every single picture. I observe these changes in the life of the world as if I received their explanation from above; what oppresses others elevates me more and more, inspires and fortifies me. How can you want me to accuse destiny to complain about people and curse them? Destiny—I laugh at it; as for men they are too ignorant and too enslaved for me to be annoyed by them.' " The religious overtone in this singular confession is not lost on Trotsky, for he declares, "Despite their slight savor of ecclesiastical eloquence those are fine words. I subscribe to them."[1]

The Marxian faith that the "objective" conditions of history support the moral purpose of the proletarian extends even to the hope that his enemies will defeat themselves, an analogue to the Christian idea that God will "use the wrath of man to praise him." The belief of Marx that "when the proletariat proclaims the dissolution of the existing order of things it is merely announcing the secret of its own existence for it is itself the virtual dissolution of this order of things" is an effort of the religious imagination to snatch victory from defeat, and runs parallel

[1]Leon Trotsky, *My Life,* p. 582.

129

to the Christian hope that "the last shall be first and the first last." There is certainly something more than a sober analysis of economic and political facts in the Marxian paradoxes. Economic facts may give them a measure of support; but economic facts as such never disclose a moral purpose or meaning if the moral imagination does not read the meaning into them. In this case the moral imagination finds exactly that meaning in them which will make the impossible (the victory of the proletariat) seem possible and which will therefore nerve the protagonists of the impossible ideal with the courage supplied by an indomitable hope. The Marxian has a secularized version of the religious assurance, "Fear not, little flock, it is your Father's good pleasure to give you the kingdom."

The analogy between Marxian religion and the more classical religious faith is further revealed in the fact that it has the same difficulty, revealed in the history of Christian thought, in striking a proper balance between voluntarism and determinism. The idea that the downfall of capitalism is inevitable is as powerful an incentive to moral energy as was Calvinistic determinism in the heyday of Calvinistic faith. The belief that determinism inevitably leads to an inclination to take "moral holidays" (William James) is a typical illusion of a rationalistic and individualistic age. On the contrary, men develop the highest energy in the pursuit of a moral or social goal when they are most certain that they are affirming the preordained "counsels of God."

Nevertheless there are perils of fatalism in every deterministic theory and they are revealed in Marxian as well as in Christian thought and practice. When the attainment of an historical goal is regarded as preordained it may nerve the early small flock of faith to tireless energy and yet tempt the later church to a sleepy fatalism. The German parliamentary-revolutionary socialism elaborated by Kautsky succumbed to this temptation; against it and similar tendencies Lenin insisted: "Some revolutionists attempt to prove that there is absolutely no way out of a crisis. That is an error. There does not exist a position from which there is absolutely no way out." Lenin's insistence that the objective forces of history must be consciously directed toward a revolutionary goal by a revolutionary class seeks to preserve a proper "dialectic" balance between "religious" determinism and the voluntarism of an adequate moral theory.

In the opinion of Max Eastman[2] Lenin has completely revised the "mystical" determinism of Marx in the actual practice of his statesmanship while he clings to remnants of it in theory. Eastman regards these remnants as inconsistent with Lenin's

[2]Max Eastman, *Marx and Lenin.*

dominant interpretation; but Eastman is an intellectual communist who does not understand the function of religious determinism in generating moral energy. There is enough pure determinism in the thought of Lenin to prompt modern Leninists (as for instance the official communist party of America) to criticize Sidney Hook's interpretation of the Marxian dialectic, as erring on the side of ascribing too much significance to conscious affirmation of a determined historical goal, and to ascribe this defect to Dewey's influence upon Hook.[3] These controversies repeat many of the old controversies of Christian theology and illustrate the paradoxical relation of religion to morality. Religious hope always tends to encourage moral energy by promising victory to a seemingly hopeless moral enterprise, but it also enervates moral energy by guaranteeing victory too unreservedly. Generally the vital period of a religion extracts resources of energy from its hope while the later more conventional eras use it to escape responsibility for action.

The Marxian mythology belongs to the general category of Jewish apocalypticism in distinction to the Hellenistic interpretations of life and history. In Greek thought the centre of life's meaning is always found in the passionless forms of reason which are conceived as transcending history and to which the

[3]Sidney Hook, *Toward an Understanding of Karl Marx.*

individual may escape from the confusions of history both in this life and in an immortal life to come. In Jewish religion there is always the hope that history itself will be redeemed and that spirit will reduce its confusions to order and harmony. While Christian orthodoxy has on the whole followed Greek rather than Jewish thought, Jesus himself, the early church with its hope for the parousia, and the various millenarian sects of Christian history, have been truer to the Jewish interpretation of the relation of spirit to nature and have lived by the hope that history itself was to be redeemed. Broadly speaking, the difference between the two is the difference between those who regard the issues of life from the perspective of the individual conscience and those who are immersed in a social situation and therefore desire not individual emancipation from history's injustices, but the achievement of justice in history. That is why the Christian sects of the disinherited, who had something of the Marxian proletarian's feeling for the social situation, turned to Jewish and early Christian apocalypse to express their religious faith. On the other hand theologians like Dean Inge are significantly both Platonists and protagonists of social conservatism.

There are naturally important differences as well as similarities between Christian apocalypticism and the Marxian hope. The Jewish-Christian eschatology

133

demands of the devotee that he purge himself of the sins and injustices of society, and await and aid the coming of the kingdom of righteousness by repentance, love and prayer. It does not permit participation in the vengeance of history; for such participation involves the soul anew in historic injustice. "Vengeance is mine, I will recompense, saith the Lord." This is the dominant motif not only in the thought of Jesus, but also in that of the Second Isaiah, from which he drew much of his inspiration, and in the faith of a Tolstoi or the religion of sects like the Mennonites. If applied with complete consistency such faith prevents the believer from participating in the very historical processes which are regarded as God's way of bringing evil to naught. It affirms that there is moral meaning in the self-defeat of evil in the world and yet is prevented by moral scruples from joining in the movements of history through which the defeat of evil is finally executed. In its absolutely pure form such faith must finally express itself in pure apocalypticism, and depend upon God to change human nature through some miraculous transformation in order that pure spirit and pure love may triumph in the world of history.

The faith that nature will be transformed into super-nature without being transported to a trans-historical realm is rather too pure to be held by any great number of people. In the history of Christian thought it has therefore always been diluted either by Greek dualism which separated the world of spirit from the world of nature and history, and expected the perfect victory of the spirit only in the trans-historical realm, or by modern naturalistic monism, which hoped for the gradual and evolutionary victory of the ethical in nature and history itself. Christian orthodoxy has chosen the former compromise and liberal Christianity has chosen the second. Neither of them is in any sense morally preferable to a possible compromise between the Marxian and the pure Christian mythology. If Christianity is to survive this era of social disintegration and social rebuilding, and is not to be absorbed in or annihilated by the secularized religion of Marxism it must come to terms with the insights of Marxist mythology. There is truth in this mythology because it is more able to affirm the moral meaning in contemporary chaos than orthodox Christianity, since the latter tends to regard all history as unredeemed and unredeemable chaos. It is superior to liberal Christianity because Christian liberalism is spiritually dependent upon bourgeois liberalism and is completely lost when its neat evolutionary process toward an ethical historical goal is suddenly engulfed in a social catastrophe.

While Christianity must come to terms with Marxian mythology it cannot afford to capitulate to it. To do so means that the distinction between spirit and nature, established in pure Christianity, is lost, and Marxism thereby betrays the ethical enterprise into an illusion, akin to the liberal illusion; for it believes that a kingdom of pure love can be established in history and that its vindictive justice will be transmuted into pure justice. Such a faith destroys the tension between the demands of spirit and the impulses of nature without which man cannot aspire to the highest humanity. The tension between spirit and nature must remain to the end of history lest the impulses of nature clothe themselves with the moral prestige of the spiritual and secure a moral immunity behind which they express themselves without moral restraint.

XI

THE EXECUTORS OF JUDGMENT

XI

THE EXECUTORS OF
JUDGMENT

I T is not easy to discover a moral logic in history.
Yet amidst the confusion of its

> "Deaths for the right cause, deaths for
> wrong cause,
> Pæans of victory and groans of defeat"

it is possible to discern the logic of an inexorable
judgment upon evil. The mighty are cast from their
seats and those of low degree are exalted when the
evils of the mighty have reached proportions great
enough to excite the spirit of resistance among the
lowly. The moral logic of history is never pure and
dispassionate precisely because judgment upon evil
cannot be executed without stiffening the spirit of
justice with an alloy of the spirit of vengeance. If
the life of collective man were completely rational
those who commit evil would repent of it and those
who suffer from evil would temper their vindictive
passions with the spirit of forgiveness. Unfortunately only a small proportion of those who commit social
evil are capable of repentance and likewise only a few
among those who suffer from it are able to develop a

corresponding spirit of objective justice. The stubbornness with which social evil is maintained requires that the force which is to dislodge it be propelled by the impulses of nature as well as the ideals of the spirit, by vengeance as well as by justice. The executors of judgment in history are always driven by both hunger and dreams, by both the passions of warfare and the hope for a city of God.

This is why history progresses toward the higher good by very tortuous routes and why the dreams of the ideal are sometimes cruelly disappointed. To put the matter in terms of specific history: The cruelties of Czardom are avenged by the furor of a communism which so mixes creative and moral elements in its enterprise with so many primeval passions and so many of the old cruelties inverted that only a very objective and sympathetic observer can discern what is good in the welter or what is evil. It must therefore always be the purpose of those who try, in a measure, to guide the course of history to check the desperate brutalities of a dying civilization in order that the new which emerges may not be too completely corrupted and blinded by the spirit of vengeance.

Nevertheless only the detached rationalist and moralist will ever hope or imagine that the judgments of history will be pronounced and executed by bewigged judges who stand above the conflicts and passions of history and are thus able to make nice calculations and discriminations of the good and evil, always so hopelessly interlaced in the living reality of social life. In brief, the judges of history are always barbarians, whether they be Teutonic hordes, beating at the gates of Rome, mediæval tradesmen and townsmen whose commercial argosies destroyed the power of the lord in his castle, or modern proletarians, intent upon an equalitarian and collectivist society. Perhaps it is the unique feature of modern society that these barbarians should be bred within and not without the gates of civilization. Society having withheld its cultural advantages from them and having disciplined them in physical hardihood by denying its physical comforts and securities to them, will thus have created the very vigor and primitive vitality by which judgment is executed. The new barbarians may lack a proper appreciation of the achievements of culture and art with which every effete civilization adorns itself and hides the nakedness of its lusts.

Something valuable must therefore always be lost when barbarians destroy a civilization. But, since highly elaborated civilizations always hide, more than they check, the brutal impulses of life, the unashamed brutalities of the barbarian invaders are never without a measure of moral gain. They at least substitute honesty for hypocrisy. Just as the trader who defeated the landed aristocrat was not actually but only more patently greedy than the latter, so the modern proletarian who will destroy the civilization of the business man is not actually but only more honestly brutal than the commercialist and industrialist. At each new turn in history what has been covered is revealed; and one can never be quite certain whether life has actually become more brutal because the inhibition of traditional restraints has been momentarily broken or whether we merely see collective human behavior as it really is without the veiling devices of social ritual, traditional amenities and proper form.

Whatever may be the loss or gain to "eternal" values in this invasion or revolt of the barbarians, their victory is as certain as their revolt is inevitable when the time is ripe. Conventionally nice people have always held up their hands in horror at the processes of "rough justice" through which and in which history moves forward. But conventionally nice people who live leisured lives at the price of other men's toil do not have as pure moral judgments as they imagine. What is more important, they lack the physical force to execute their moral judgments. In the important crises of history moral judgments are executed only if they are supported by some force of nature, since history never moves upon the purely moral plane.

The victory of the barbarians is certain not only because they have physical advantages over the less robust defenders of the old regime but also because they can add certain moral advantages to their physical strength and their strategic resources. Their chief moral advantage consists in tho fact that they are tated to contend for a society which the logic of history affirms. Their equalitarianism may be derived from their own interests but it will benefit the whole of society. While it would be foolish to believe that any society will ever realize complete equality it is nevertheless true that equal justice is a perennial moral need and a contemporary economic necessity of society. It is a moral need because both excessive privilege (particularly privilege unrelated to social function) and excessive penury are destructive of the highest human values. "Give me neither poverty nor riches, fill me with the food that is needful for me," is a prayer which still states a basic condition of moral and spiritual health. The urgent immediate economic need for equal justice has been previously considered. Without greater equality in the distribution of wealth a technical civilization cannot live. For this reason the proletarian ideal of equality, while arising from the peculiar interests of the disinherited, actually affirms moral and social values which transcend the interests of any class.

Moral advantages do not always guarantee the victory of a cause in history. Since history is constructed by forces of nature as well as spirit there is no guarantee that in any specific instance might may not prevail. Nevertheless there is genuine historical and social power in moral advantages. In the long run the class, nation or group which cannot maintain the loyalty of its ethically most sensitive members loses important strength in the social struggle. The fact is that no new force has ever been able to establish itself in history if it has not been able to win a considerable degree of support from its enemies by moral suasion before the issue between the old and the new was finally joined.

Yet social struggles are never decided purely by rational and moral force. The physical advantages of the disinherited are therefore of real moment. There are two distinct types of such advantages. The first consists in the physical hardihood of people who live close to the margin of subsistence and are therefore accustomed to hardships and privations, and capable of physical courage and initiative. Extreme poverty may of course rob the workers of this advantage. Actual hunger and malnutrition may sap the physical foundations of martial courage. That is why the Marxian theory of "increasing misery" as the basis of revolutionary ardor may be interpreted in terms untrue to the actual facts. Revolutionary ardor arises when physical need destroys caution and begets desperation. But actual hunger may enervate rebellious heroism.

The rise of German fascism proves that the impoverished middle classes may actually excel the manual workers both in the capacity to undergo physical hardships for the sake of a political cause and in the determination to achieve their own political objectives. The defeat of the trade unions by the superior morale and martial ardor of the bourgeois "storm troops" of Hitler's army is an instructive chapter in modern history. It proves that in nations, in which the middle classes have reached the strength to which they have attained in the western world, the manual worker is not the only force which imperils the old order. At the moment these lower middle classes are politically confused and are inclined to defend the old economic order for fear that its destruction will entail the annihilation of cultural and national values which they highly prize. But already they are being merged with the manual workers in the armies of fascism. When the final issues are joined the holders of privilege will receive little support from them. And they will share with the worker the courage which is prompted by desperation, the patience which has been born of years of privation and the martial strength which rests on physical energy. Against the disinherited, whether they be middle class or proletarian, those who have been softened by privilege cannot avail, once the political issues have been transferred from parliament to marching armies, as is the case in Germany today and will

145

probably be the case in every nation when the disintegration of the old order has proceeded far enough.

The other physical advantage which the disinherited hold is their control of the vast machinery of modern civilization. Other classes may own the machines and their legal property rights may give them advantages as long as the social order, in which these rights have prestige, holds. But when the moment of dissolution comes events are no longer determined by traditional rights but by strategic social power. The power held by those who perform the services of society, who man the machines, and who keep the wheels in motion must be regarded as highly strategic. Oswald Spengler, the brilliant protagonist of social reaction, believes that this power of the worker must ultimately seal the doom of the privileged social classes.[1] While Spengler looks forward to this eventuality with melancholy forebodings, the champions of the laborer's creative capacities are able to extract high hopes from his prophecy that the owners of machines will not finally be able to avail against the power of those who actually manipulate the technical process of modern society.[2] The future belongs to the worker. He will become the ultimate arbiter of destiny in a technical civilization because he is armed with a combination of physical strength, technical

[1]*Cf.* Oswald Spengler, *Man and Technics.*
[2]*Cf.* Ernst Juenger, *Der Arbeiter, Herrschaft und Gestalt.*

efficiency and moral purpose. Against that combination of strategic power traditional privileges can maintain themselves only as long as they have the prestige which established order confers. Once that order disintegrates and an old social equilibrium is overturned, it is certain that in the establishment of a new one political power will be arrogated by those who possess the most significant social power. That is as certain as the fact that soldiers ruled society in a military age and property owners ruled it in the most recent past. We may deprecate or welcome that fact but we can hardly deny its inevitability.

The inevitability of the reign of the workers proves nothing in regard either to the time which will be required to establish it or the possible benefits which mankind may derive from it. The barbarian revolt against or invasion of a civilization is never an unmixed blessing. But upon that problem we shall have more to say. As regards the time which will be required to make the inevitable actual, prophecy is foolish and dangerous. No one can say how well the various artifices and devices, by which the present social order is attempting to postpone or to avert its doom, may succeed. Another world war seems practically inevitable. But it is not at all certain when it will come. Unemployment appears to be a chronic disease of the present system which would undermine its prestige even if a world war did not shatter it.

147

But no one can say to what degree the present rulers will be able to mitigate the evils of unemployment and thus postpone the final day of reckoning.

Furthermore it must be remembered that those who are destined to become the rulers of society are deficient in tactical skill, however great may be their advantages in significant power. Only occasionally do they have a strategic genius of the resourcefulness and resoluteness of a Lenin to command their cause. A society based on privilege tends to attract the ablest minds to its standards by the immediate and concrete prizes which it is able to offer. It is even able to tempt, beguile and cajole many whose youth was devoted to the proletarian cause. Those who will ultimately rule modern society will therefore suffer many defeats before they finally triumph. Sometimes they will be outmanœuvred by their more skillful opponents and sometimes they will be betrayed in the house of their friends. History never moves, even to its inevitable goals, on a straight line. As an example one need only to think of the tremendous difference in tempo and diversity in method in which bourgeois democracy triumphed in France, England and Germany. Nevertheless the proletarian seems as certain to rule a new civilization as it is that the commercial and industrial owner held the significant power in the social order which is passing.

XII

NEITHER VOTES NOR BULLETS

NEITHER VOTES NOR BULLETS

THE political power in any society is held by the group which commands the most significant type of non-political power, whether it be military prowess, priestly prestige, economic ownership or the ability to manipulate the technical processes of the community. If the governing group is able to add to this possession of power an implicit confidence in itself as the rightful government, a high morale and a sure sense of direction it is able to win the consent of the rest of the community to its rule and maintain it without challenge. The governing group either believes itself to be or tries, at least, to create the illusion that it is, ordained, either by some mystical "divine right" or by an only slightly less mystical "consent of the governed," to hold the reins of power in society and to symbolize the unity of the nation. The ability of a governing group to transmute its specialized non-political power into political power depends upon the plausibility of its claim to government and the willingness of society to accept the claim.

A government is thus never created either by the pure consent of the governed or by the sheer use of military power. The democratic idealists who imagine that the ballot actually creates the basis of political power and the conservative or radical "Realpolitiker" who thinks of it only in terms of military or other forms of martial strength are equally mistaken in analyzing the true basis of political strength. The ballot never determines which class is to govern a community. It may determine which faction of a class is to govern, whether Whig or Tory, Democrat or Republican. Or it may be a convenient method of registering the degree to which the general community accepts or rejects the governing class's assertion of the right to govern. On occasion, as in the municipal elections preceding the Spanish Revolution, an election may prove to a governing class that it has lost the loyalty of the community and may persuade it to abdicate before it is forcibly eliminated. The vote is in effect an indication of the comparative strength of the military power which might be arrayed against the rulers if they should hold to their rule until the issues are joined in final combat.

Since, however, political power rests upon the double pillars of force and consent, and since force is sometimes able to win a reluctant consent, it is natural that governing groups should usually refuse to abdicate when they have discovered that they have lost the loyalty of the community. They can always hope that the force which they still hold will be able to re-establish the respect and loyalty of the community. They hardly ever realize that force is effective only when the fear of force is mixed with reverence for it and that reverence is dissipated when undue force is used. In spite of this difficulty it is possible for governments to hold themselves for a time by force alone, particularly if their opponents are not united. If opposition from various directions should create an equilibrium of forces, even an unpopular government could maintain itself for some time by pure police power at the centre of a vortex. Radicals as well as conservatives may make mistakes in estimating the significance of force in government and imagine that the capture of significant centres of political power will establish their rule. They do not always realize that a new governing force can finally maintain itself only if its program and purpose is in general accord with the needs and ethos of a community so that the right to govern may achieve plausibility in the total community.

The recognition of the limits of force in government must not tempt the political theorist to adopt the opposite fallacy of the pure democratic faith and imagine that government is created and maintained purely by rational persuasion. The consent of the governed never creates a government. The withdrawal of consent may destroy governments; but the factor of consent does not create governments because the general public is never able to conceive political programs or fashion political strategies. It can only say yes or no to various alternatives presented to it. The public as such is without organs of conscious direction. Nor is there any process which would give a community a natural organ of self-direction. These organs may partly grow out of the community but they are partly imposed upon it. In a period of stability this is not recognized because the governing group has been merged into the general community and its direction of affairs therefore seems to belong to the whole community. In reality the alternatives of government policy are always initiated by some small and cohesive group, whose social functions are important enough to give it prestige in a considerable portion of the community and the opportunity to make its claim of government over the total community seem plausible.

The technique of democracy has had greater than these limited possibilities ascribed to it because it has been successfully used to arbitrate between various factions in the governing classes and to decide between minor alternatives within the general scheme of a given social and political order. The vote which determined whether Whigs or Tories should rule in England was not a vote which decided between differ-

ing social systems but between the landed and industrial sections of the economic owners. Similarly the
contest between Republicans and Democrats in
America was originally a conflict between the urban
and the pioneer factions of bourgeois democracy.
More recently issues have become so confused that
neither party represents any clearly defined section
of the community or presents stable alternatives in
policy. At any rate political contests between such
parties do not involve the question of the right of a
particular class to rule society. In England the actual political power has remained in the hands of the
landed gentry and industrial wealth, while in America a combination of industrialists and farmers has
created a democracy, slightly more bourgeois and less
aristocratic than the English variety. If a new class
in society, as labor for instance, endeavors to avail
itself exclusively of the instruments of democracy to
join the issue between two distinct social classes it
may lose its morale in the effort to insinuate a new
governing force into old governing forms or it discovers that the old governing forms can be used to
frustrate its efforts. The British Labor party has
had both experiences.

The technique of democracy can arbitrate only between minor alternatives in governmental policy because democracy assumes the readiness of a minority
to acquiesce in the program of a victorious ma-

jority. If such acquiescence is withheld the majority is forced to use either police or military power in subjugating the minority and a political struggle becomes a military one. The acquiescence of a minority is usually withheld if the political issues which a society faces actually involve the substitution of a new social system for an old one, because such a substitution means that the traditional right of one group to govern is challenged by another group. Such a challenge means that all the presuppositions which a society has taken for granted are called in question. When the alternatives which confront a society are wider than those which can be derived from old presuppositions and traditions, the new alternative will be presented with greater vigor than a democratic process allows for and the old one will be defended with a desperate courage supplied by both fear of extinction and a sense of righteous defense of the eternal sanctities.

It is idle for this reason to hope that modern society will ever make the transition from capitalism to socialism by purely democratic processes, akin to those which have served modern nations in deciding between various alternatives within the general scheme of capitalism. The issue between capitalism and socialism not only challenges the accepted political traditions of centuries but it contemplates the substitution of the worker for the economic owner as the real bearer of political power. Ultimately it envisages a society in which technical skill rather than economic ownership will be the basis of the most significant social and therefore political power. This latter point is obscured in socialist ideology because the touch of romanticism in socialist thought allows for the illusion that there will be no oligarchy in the new society.

The contest between socialism and capitalism is therefore a political conflict between social classes so divergent in interest, ethos and political purpose and between social objectives so contradictory and mutually exclusive that the pure methods of democracy will never suffice to arbitrate the conflict. They will be used and they ought to be used as far as possible. They will determine to what degree the governing group has lost the confidence of the general community in its right to organize society; and the skirmishes on the purely political battlefield will be used to strengthen the morale, discipline and numerical strength of the group which aspires to government. They may even grant the neutral and semi-neutral social groups an opportunity to survey the issues dispassionately and to give one or the other side its support. The longer democratic methods of arbitration hold out the more will society be spared unnecessary conflict and chaos.

It may be prophesied with almost dogmatic certainty that they will not hold out to the final crisis because it would be contrary to nature if an old governing group capitulated without exhausting every resource at its disposal to maintain itself; and among those resources there are always sources of strength other than the mere weight of democratic numbers. It would be equally unnatural if the challenging group did not draw upon all of its available resources in the final struggle. Such a struggle is bound to be long and tortuous because the two groups command incommensurate types of social power which, as we have seen, are not easily joined in battle. The one group possesses the power derived from the traditional rights accorded economic owners. The other group has the physical and (if technicians are included) the intellectual skill to manipulate the modern technical process. A struggle between two such groups is like a battle between two armies in which the one uses staves and the other stones. The advancing group achieves morale through the knowledge that it possesses the most significant type of power in modern society. The retreating group, though it has lost some morale, is nevertheless armed with the confidence supplied by traditional sanctions. The battle between them will be indecisive for decades because the weapons are so disparate. Yet in the hour of crisis both will probably use the same weapons. For the weapons of physical combat are finally available for both groups (though the side with the most men will have the fewest guns) and these weapons are resorted to in the end if a social issue is not solved by more democratic or pacific means.

The group character of political conflict has not been fully realized by modern observers because their individualism persuaded them to view a national society as comprised of individuals who had no other loyalty but their national allegiance. The commercial and industrial oligarchy which controls this national society is even capable of deceiving itself about its real character to such a degree that it feels an honest abhorrence of the class doctrines of the workers, even though the workers only avow frankly what is implicit in the actions and beliefs of the owning group.

The complexity of modern society, which creates intermediary social groups between those holding the actual social power and the rebellious workers, further confuses the picture. The professional middle classes, the small traders, and the farmers are not immediately involved in the titanic conflict between owners and workers, and their multifarious political attitudes may therefore create the illusion that a national society is composed of mere individuals. Furthermore the owners and the workers are both the victims of a mechanical civilization in which organic relations are not easily achieved and they therefore fail to realize an effective social cohesion until the conflict between them forces each into social solidarity.

In America the workers are still without any real organ or centre of cohesion. They are merely resentful and dissatisfied individuals and have not risen to the status of a self-conscious and coherent group. There are American democratic idealists who think this is an advantage and believe that it proves the superior merits of American democracy and the legitimacy of its equalitarian and classless pretensions. They will discover in time that all historic political issues are settled in group conflict and that no new political ideal can ever be victorious if it is not borne by a highly self-conscious and determined group.

Fundamental political issues, such as the conflict between capitalism and socialism, are therefore in reality battles between conflicting social wills. The issues will be ultimately determined by the comparative strength of these competing collective wills. The counting of votes in democratic fashion and a possible martial combat are both incidental to this struggle of wills. Votes may determine to what degree either group has lost or gained general support; and a physical combat may test the courage with which either group is ready to defend its position by the actual sacrifice of life. But a victory or defeat either at the polls or in war need not be decisive. Triumph will finally rest upon the banners of the group whose will is most steady and determined. This steadiness and determination must grow out of a strong sense of mission, confidence in the possibility of ultimate triumph and the possession of a leadership which knows how to give coherence and direction to the will of the group and which uses strategic skill in advancing the group's objectives.

If will-power is the determining factor it is as certain that the laborer will be victorious over the owner as that his victory will be long delayed. His victory is certain because the logic of history demands his type of society rather than the one which the owner is trying to preserve and because he possesses more significant social power than that of ownership. He therefore possesses advantages both in the sources of his morale and in strategic weapons. But his victory will be delayed because the owners have a morale which traditional social concepts support and this morale will be broken only gradually. The morale of the working class on the other hand can be developed only as it gradually becomes fully conscious of its destiny and of the potential strength with which it is endowed to fulfill its destiny. It cannot become fully conscious of its mission and its power without a leadership profound enough to understand the logic of history and astute enough to develop a statesmanlike strategy. This combination of tactical skill and re-

ligious and philosophical profundity is extremely
rare. It may be for this reason that a new society,
such as the workers are destined to build, will have to
wait until just the right type of leadership emerges.
The revolutionary class may suffer many defeats
before its ultimate triumph, because its social coherence has not become sufficiently intense and because
its leadership is wanting either in strategic skill or
in intellectual depth.

XIII

THE PERIL OF BARBARISM IN THE
SPIRIT OF VENGEANCE

THE PERIL OF BARBARISM IN THE SPIRIT OF VENGEANCE

A DYING civilization invites the perils of barbarism, whether it dies prematurely at the hands of its barbarian foes or whether it tries to perpetuate itself beyond its day. If it is destroyed by a political group which has the power to give the deaththrust to a moribund social system but lacks the morale and the unity to establish a new social order, our various industrial nations may have to submit to the anarchy of prolonged civil conflict before a stable order is established. If the attempt to perpetuate a dying system beyond its day is made (and the indications are that we are already witnessing such an effort) an essentially international economic order will disintegrate into its various national units, each of which will try to establish a self-sufficing economy. This fascist economic nationalism will imperil the life and security of the millions of people who have been added to the population of the industrial nations since the Industrial Revolution. It will increase manufacturing costs and thereby lower living standards. Culturally it will be as inimical to a free exchange of ideas as it is to the free exchange of goods. It will corrupt the culture of the western world with excessive nationalistic passions. Modern fascist Germany is providing an instructive lesson in what the complete governmental control of all organs of propaganda and education is able to accomplish in prostituting a general culture to purely nationalistic ends. It can create an atmosphere of hysteria in which only a few of the bravest and most sensitive spirits continue to think clearly on the issues which confront our civilization.

Thus a social system which tries to outlive its day may result in the barbarism of international anarchy, penury and cultural confusion. It may be that nothing but the horrors of another international war, toward which this kind of anarchy tends, will finally dissolve the living death of such a civilization.[1]

[1]Summing up his exhaustive survey of the contemporary political situation in *International Politics,* Professor Frederick L. Schuman speculates on the possibilities of barbarism in the future in the following interesting and convincing prophecy:

"The central problem of the twentieth century is this: can the individualistic societies and bourgeois governments of the western nation-states renounce uncontrolled acquisitive capitalism and the diplomacy of power, profits and prestige to a sufficient degree to prevent the dissolution of the world in which they live? Can they achieve world unity and the social direction of economic activity before they are overwhelmed by the forces which have created the present order and now threaten that order with destruction? These questions call urgently for answer in the immediate future. Upon the answer hinges the whole future of western civilization and the Western State System. And a negative answer, in all probability, will not mean a mere tedious continuation into the indefinite future of the present muddling and fumbling and befuddled confusion. It means rather a progressive and accelerated disintegration of

On the other hand there are also perils of barbarism in the premature dissolution of a social system at the hands of its barbarian foes. These perils are not those usually feared by the defenders of the *status quo* and arising from the barbarian's lack of the softer virtues and amenities which adorn a stable civilization. Since the moralities of an effete culture are always something of "whited sepulchres, which indeed appear beautiful outward, but are within full of dead men's bones and of all uncleanness," there are always cleansing possibilities in the robust virilities of the barbarian. The real peril of barbarism arises from the fact that the victims of injustice are always actuated by the spirit of vengeance as much as by the spirit of justice. This is inevitable but it is also dangerous. It is inevitable because it is impossible for large masses of men to resent injustice as injustice. They resent the injustice which is done to them. The modern proletarian is motivated to a certain

the world economy and a relapse of the western world into international anarchy, war and suicidal combat between imperial powers.—Out of the chaos may emerge universal social revolution, universal destruction of old ways of life by a world rebellion of the industrial proletariat and the colonial subject peoples.— Eventually life in the western world may be resumed at something like its old level with a new ideology, a new mythology, a new set of social relationships, economic patterns and political institutions adequate to the exigencies of a mechanized world community. Or—and the other alternative is quite probable—western mankind may slip down into a long and bloody decline at the end of which the whole fabric of the world economy will have been shattered and those who survive will be reduced to ruder and more primitive modes of living, which will seem barbarous and brutish by comparison to the vanished golden age of capitalism and nationalism." P. 849.

167

degree by the spirit of pure justice. His dreams of an ideal social order in which no one will suffer from injustice are proof of that. But he inclines to identify the specific evils from which he suffers with the principle of evil itself, and to dramatize himself as the pure instrument of justice. He thereby reveals the egoistic elements in his spirit of justice, the very elements which change justice into vindictiveness.

The profounder aspects of the moral problem of humanity escape this egoism. It is not recognized that human society has a perpetual conflict with the egoism of individuals and groups. This fact is obscured by the proletarian's identification of capitalistic injustice with the very evil of injustice. There is correspondingly no sympathy or pity for human life as such. "Man as such," declares Maurice Hindus, in writing about Russian communism, "evokes neither respect nor sympathy. Emphasis is always on social origin, not on what a man is but what his father was and did."[2] Here is a clear indication of the inversion of the aristocratic principle in communism and a perfect illustration of how the spirit of vengeance easily substitutes one form of injustice for another.

The fact that the egoistic and vindictive element in the spirit of justice is not recognized is the very basis of its excessive cruelty. It feels itself morally justified in exterminating its foes because it is under the

[2]Maurice Hindus, *The Great Offensive*, p. 181.

illusion that such a course will eliminate injustice. It thereby gains a moral prestige in its own conscience for the expression of an uncritical egoism. Thus the communist can be ruthless in "liquidating" his "class enemies," the kulaks for instance, and in including among his class enemies every one who does not see eye to eye with him. The extension of the term "kulak," originally intended to designate rich peasant usurers, so that it now includes every peasant who resists the communist program of collectivization is an interesting example of how cruel the spirit of vengeance may be when it has gained the moral prestige of the spirit of justice. Egoism sees only the injustice which the other has committed upon the individual or the collective self. It imagines itself free of the temptation to injustice and therefore indulges in the illusion that elimination of the foe will guarantee future justice. While there are greater moral possibilities in a class struggle than in international conflict because there is actually more justice on the one side than the other, the hope that the victory of an exploited class will automatically establish a just society is almost as pathetic as the perennial desire of, let us say, France and Germany to achieve "justice" by avenging the wrong which the other has committed upon it in a previous decade, a desire which involves the two nations in an endless round of vengeance and injustice.

The spirit of vengeance is necessarily cruel because it is blind to the similarity of the evil in the self and in the other. It does not recognize the peril of injustice as inhering in the egoism which is common to all mankind. All decent pity for the weaknesses of others is prompted by a contrite recognition of the possibilities of the same sin in the self. "Let him who is without sin cast the first stone" is an admonition which flows naturally from the profound religious insight which judges all human actions with the criterion of an absolute standard of love, and finds them all defective. If applied with complete rigor it will regard all human actions equally defective and thereby make relative judgments upon historic evil impossible. Hence every great passion for a greater measure of social justice in history will find the criteria of a religion, proceeding from a completely transcendent perspective, dangerous. This fact discloses one reason for the communist animus against religion.

While a religion holding a transcendent perspective upon moral actions may actually lame moral judgments upon the historical level, where all things are relative and where distinctions between the relatively good and the relatively evil are very important, the general influence of such religious insights are necessary to qualify the spirit of vengeance and to prevent victims of injustice from dramatizing themselves as the instruments of pure justice. Whenever they do so they become capable of the same cruelties which religious fanatics of all the ages, who regarded themselves as the instruments of the divine and the absolute, have practised. Man is always most inhuman, not when he is unconsciously driven by natural impulse, but when he imagines his natural impulses and his relative values to be the instruments of some absolute good.

The impulses of nature only achieve demonic proportions when they are falsely "mixed" with spirit and gain immunity from the moral censor by appropriating the moral prestige of the spiritual. The bourgeois democrats of the nineteenth century were able to ride roughshod over their foes because they believed that the principles of democracy for which they fought had universal validity. History has proved their faith to have been mistaken and has revealed democratic principles to have been screens for middle-class interests. History may also prove the proletarian to be mistaken in his belief that he is the herald and the author of the final form of civilization. A class which possesses no privileges and which seeks to abolish all special privileges in society has the right to claim that its ideals transcend its interests; but it will have difficulty in realizing that some of its viewpoints are nevertheless partial to the time and place from which they sprang.

The vigor with which the Russian communist subordinates the peasant to the interests of a collectivized industrial society is an interesting example of the unconscious imperialism of a group expressing itself in devotion to what it regards a universal principle. The communists are certain that they are collectivizing the peasants for the latter's own good and their measures against peasant opposition therefore reveal the cruelty which always characterizes the will-to-power of righteous people who are certain that they are the instruments of a righteous cause. It has not occurred to them that some peasant opposition may spring from deep-rooted instincts of the man of the soil and that these instincts have their own validity in competition with those of urban man.

The passion for both collectivization and industrialization of the modern Russian communist is a characteristic urban attitude. The former is justified by the necessities of urban technology; but it is not certain that the agrarian problem demands the same degree of collectivization as the urban one. The passion for mechanization is justified in as far as it supplants inefficient with efficient agricultural tools; but if it is carried to the degree of destroying peasant handcraft and art, as has actually been the case, it represents a vulgar urban passion for technology and a blindness to treasures of the spirit, revealed in the peasant's ancient arts and unknown to the modern urban man.

That the peasant, who has for centuries defended his ancient culture with its emphasis upon family, religion, handcraft and self-sufficient serenity against the encroachments of capitalistic urbanism, should be forced to capitulate so completely to communistic urbanism in Russia is an interesting example of the force of unconscious imperialism in a proletarian class which regards itself the instrument of the final and the ideal society.

The egoistic element in the communist spirit of justice is also apparent in the uncompromising attitude toward all cultural and other values which are associated in any way with the bourgeois culture and civilization against which communism is rebelling. Romantic conceptions of marriage are regarded as bourgeois aberrations and as a result the effort is made to reduce the family to the barest biological proportions. The sentiment of nationalism, so often a tool in the hands of capitalism to hide and to perpetuate injustice, is for this reason condemned as an irrationality of fools which invites the manipulation of knaves. Religion is placed with the same unqualified dogmatism in the category of reaction. "Never did the idea of God relate the individual to society," declares Lenin. "It always related the oppressed classes to the faith in the divinity of their oppressors. . . . There was a time in history when in spite of this origin and this actual significance of the idea of

173

God, the struggle for democracy and the proletariat went on in the struggle of one religious idea against another. These times have long since passed. At present in Europe and in Russia every apology or justification of the idea of God, even the most subtle, the most well intended, is a justification for reaction." The indiscriminating dogmatism of these words is a typical product of the spirit of vindictiveness. Any symbol, value or instrument which has served the foe is identified with the sin which the foe has committed and hatred toward it is enjoined upon the faithful. It has not occurred to this kind of vindictive dogmatism that the foe (in this case the capitalist) may have appreciated certain values and treasures of history and culture not because he is a capitalist but because he is a man.

The perils of barbarism which arise from extreme vindictiveness on the part of the modern proletarian instruments of justice are twofold. It may lead to the building of a society in which perennial human values are foolishly suppressed until, by tortuous routes and means, they are able to establish themselves again. Any one who looks at human history with dispassionate eyes can be quite certain that some elements in human culture which modern Russia is trying to destroy will find their way back into its life again. Since this is the case one might be tempted to view their futile momentary suppression with a cer-

tain degree of equanimity were it not for the fact
that they create a much greater peril in the immediate
situation. The egoism and vindictiveness of communism threatens the western world with decades of internecine strife because it narrows the base of the
worker's political power and limits him as the agent
of a new unity in civilization. It does this because it
alienates the poor who are not proletarian, the peasants and the poorer middle classes from the proletarian cause. No one can say how much communist
intransigeance in Russia against the peasant may
have contributed to the stubborn resistance of European peasants to communism and their consequent
identification with fascism. If the proletarian worker
insists that his characteristic attitudes on life, religion, patriotism, family and art are absolutely essential for a revolutionary movement he will succeed
only in driving other poor classes, whom capitalism
has also disinherited and who are his potential allies,
into the arms of his enemies. That is precisely what
is happening at the present time in Europe.

It cannot be maintained that the errors of radical
proletarians are solely responsible for the inclination
of the poor of the farm and petty trade to drift
toward reaction. These classes are politically unrealistic and inept. They have little understanding
for the larger issues which are involved in the disintegration of a social order. They are inclined to hold

with desperate tenacity to minimal social prestige and privilege which the overlords of a capitalistic system grant them; and their credulous minds fall an easy prey to powerful propaganda. They have nevertheless, broadly speaking, a greater identity of economic interest with the industrial poor than with the industrial and financial masters of society. This common interest is obscured if the industrial poor insist that every cultural, religious, patriotic and social attitude and value, to which the lower middle classes are attached, must be regarded as anathema in a new society.

In Russia the danger of such intransigeance was not apparent because the cultural and religious forms to which the peasants were attached were completely moribund and the middle class was practically non-existent. The peasant furthermore had an immediate need for land and peace which created a momentary identity of interest between himself and the proletarian, and relegated the profounder differences in feeling and in mental outlook to the background long enough to give the proletarian mastery of the machinery of state. This pattern of development will not be repeated in any western nation because in all of them the cultural traditions to which the middle classes cling have greater vitality, the power of these classes is more stubborn and their capacity for political cohesion and self-defense is superior to that of the Russian peasants and small Russian middle class. For that reason an intransigeant proletarian radicalism in the western world is bound to result in driving the neutral and semi-neutral, the partially sympathetic and the confused portions of the population into the enemy's camp. Since it is always a mark of true statesmanship to prevent neutral and partially sympathetic groups from augmenting the number and force of the foe, it can easily be seen that the vindictiveness of orthodox Marxism betrays it into faulty statesmanship.

These criticisms do not imply that the Marxian ought to sacrifice the central positions of his political program. The disinherited worker is fated to see the realities of the social struggle as the other classes cannot see it. His catastrophism is truer to the political realities of our era than the liberal optimism to which most of the middle classes cling and he is therefore bound to be the guiding factor in any political policy adequate to the task of social reconstruction. Marxian radicalism cannot afford to allow the dilutions of liberalism which the middle-class intellectuals try to press upon it. An adequate radical political policy must be Marxian in the essentials of political strategy. But it will have a chance of succeeding in its main political objectives only if it learns to be less vindictive in its attitude toward all social and cultural values which are historically but not constitutionally related to social and political conservatism.

Though a barbaric interregnum can be avoided only if the forces which are destined to create a new society learn how to mitigate the spirit of vengeance, it must not be assumed that it is possible to elminate vindictiveness completely. The ambition of a pure spirituality to substitute absolute justice and forgiveness for vengeance can be realized only in very limited circles, in ascetic withdrawals from the world and in disavowal of political responsibility. Political movements are always propelled by forces of nature rather than by pure idealism. Pure disinterestedness is needed to guide the conflict of interest toward the goal of a greater harmony of interest; and the spirit of forgiveness is necessary to mitigate the force of vengeance lest it result in attenuating the political forces which make for greater justice. But these purer spiritual attitudes can only qualify and cannot completely dominate the political struggle. The liberal faith that rational and moral attitudes can alone create political tendencies, springs from a lack of understanding for the power and persistence of natural impulse in social life. Wherever that power is fully understood a pure spirituality flees into the monastery and reveals its superior realism by its disavowal of political responsibility.

The task of guiding the course of history through chaos to relative order is left undone both by the liberal who does not understand historic forces and the ascetic or semi-ascetic who flees them because he does understand them. The task must be performed by those who know that the world of history is the world of nature; but who also know that the greater degree of social cohesion of which human collectives are capable involves them in perils of anarchy and self-destruction of which the world of pure nature knows nothing. They will therefore be intent upon checking natural impulse, as for instance the impulse of vengeance, so that it will be a constructive rather than a purely destructive force. They will not give themselves to the illusion that any large number of men will ever resent the injustice done to others as much as they resent the injustice from which they suffer; and they will therefore know that vindictive elements are inevitable in great historical movements. For this reason they will not detach themselves from a political cause, destined on the whole to be an instrument of justice because an alloy of vindictiveness is found in the pure gold of its passion for righteousness. Yet at the same time they will recognize the perils of blindness and cruelty in a political movement in which the elements of hatred have overmastered the purer morality.

The radical attitude toward the sentiment of nationality is one evidence of the blindness of vindictiveness. The radical knows how frequently patriotism is

179

used as a screen for social injustice and how easily nationalistic passions may be aroused to confuse profounder social issues. He is also influenced by the fact that the truly disinherited workers, who always form the spearpoint of the radical movement, are really without a country and are therefore not bound by the sentiments of the less obviously disinherited. He therefore conceives an idealism in which the class supplants the nation as the community of most significant loyalty and which envisages an ideal world community bereft of traditional national divisions. His belief that in the present moment the class deserves his loyalty more than the nation is justified but his hope that national sentiment will be destroyed in a classless world is a rationalistic romanticism which he has inherited from the age of reason.

Patriotism is a much more powerful and persistent element than the radical realizes. It can be completely disavowed only by that small portion of a population which is so completely disinherited that it has lost contact with the cultural traditions of a nation. And even this portion, the most radical workers, will revive patriotic sentiments, once they have established a state in which they believe themselves to have a stake. All the indications are that socialism will never be established in the western world by international action on the part of the workers. It will be established in each nation by the workers who have the morale and power to establish it. It is possible that, in the event of another world war, workers' parties may take simultaneous action against the policies of their governments; but the idea that an international Marxian party can force its various national units to submit to a uniform discipline and engage in an identical policy is an illusion. It is possible of realization only as long as such a party is dominated by the prestige and the financial power of one national unit, as the Third Internationale is controlled by Russian money and prestige. If the Third Internationale were genuinely international it would cease to maintain its present coerced unity of policy and program.

If socialism should be established in every western nation it would be possible to establish a higher degree of international accord than the special interests of the various national capitalistic units now make possible. But it would not be possible to have an international government in which sentiments prompted by geography, history and race would not divide the international community. There will never be a community of mankind in the sense that there is a national community. Such a community is too vague, too all-inclusive, and too bereft of the symbols by which common men comprehend the social organization of which they are a part, to arouse the intense loyalties which men are accustomed to pay their national communities. National patriotism is compounded of many ingredients. Sentimental attachment to the soil and to the familiar scene, consciousness of a common history and the force of common memories, the binding force of a common language and of the culture which is the soul of a language, all these enter into the sentiment of nationality. No new society, no matter how much it reduces national animosities, will destroy national and racial patriotism.

The hatred of the radical for sentiments which have confused the issues in which he is primarily interested therefore betrays him into a romantic internationalism which can never be completely realized and which alienates support from his cause among classes which are related to him by common economic need but which still adhere to national sentiments and loyalties to a greater degree than he does.

A more discriminating and less vindictive policy toward national sentiment need not involve the radical in submission to nationalistic loyalties where these are obviously being used to support reactionary policies. It will in fact rob the financial oligarchs of a very effective weapon and source of prestige. It will prevent them from posing as the high priests of patriotism who are protecting the temple from defiling hands.

The radical attitude toward religion is another evidence of the blindness of vindictiveness and of the faulty statesmanship resulting from such blindness. Religion is frequently a bulwark of social conservatism. Pure religion easily leads to counsels of acquiescence because it fears the cruelty and the vindictiveness which express themselves in every social movement which seeks to eliminate injustice. Traditional and institutional religion, on the other hand, tend to impart the aura of the absolute to the existing order of things and thus to convict the radical of violating eternal sanctities when he essays to destroy an existing social order. Religion is therefore always a good target for those who have learned how to puncture the illusions and pretensions of a civilization. They will inevitably discover that it is a source of confusion because it is always used to give the ambitions of a class, the prejudices of an era and the pretensions of a nation transcendent and absolute value. Yet these corruptions of religion do not do justice to its real essence.

Religion in its quintessential character is devotion to the absolute and a yearning after value and truth which transcends the partial, the relative and the historical. Since the absolute must always be symbolized in terms of the relative it leads naturally to the absolutizing of the relative, so that devotion to God comes to mean loyalty to "holy Russia" or obedience to the Jewish law, or acceptance of the prejudices of western civilization, or conformity to puritan moral

183

standards or maintenance of a capitalistic civilization. Yet religion is never exhausted in these corruptions. At its best it criticizes the relative from the vantage point of the absolute. If it is an ethical religion it will define the absolute in moral terms, love for instance, and will bring the assertion of the will-to-live in any individual or group under the criterion of the obligation to affirm all life. Something of that religious motive is in the radical devotion to a society in which all life will have equal opportunities. Without this religious motive no radical force can ever succeed; because the mere assertion of suppressed interests cannot establish these interests if the fervor of devotion to the absolute does not sanctify this assertion. Yet the religious sanctification of relative interests in the spiritual life of the radical is, however necessary, just as dangerous a source of confusion as in conservatism. It leads to the same peril of endowing the egoism of a group or the prejudice of an era with the sanctity of the eternal.

The radical is therefore involved in the nice paradox of illustrating the universality of the religious motif in life in the very act of declaring religion to be counter-revolutionary or reactionary. The judgment by which he declares religion to be a tool of reaction is made unqualifiedly, precisely because the proletarian absolutizes spiritual attitudes which are really relative to the victims of a mechanical civilization

184

and the injustices of a capitalistic social order.

A more discriminating and less vindictive sense of justice on the part of the radical would lead to a recognition of the fact that the reactionary uses to which religion is put do not explain the nature of religion. It is of the nature of religion that it can serve both to sanctify the partial and the relative and to reveal the partiality and relativity of every specific historical project. The yearning after the absolute is what lifts humanity above the brute level. If the yearning after the absolute is easily transmuted into devotion to relative values, that weakness is due not to priestly chicane or capitalistic dishonesty but to the weakness of the human imagination. Both the virtues and vices of religion are revelations of the strength and the weakness of the spiritual in human life without regard to class or era; and both will therefore continue to reveal themselves in all human history.

If the radical could realize this more fully he could eliminate another source of weakness from his political enterprise. When he adopts an intransigeant attitude toward all religion he alienates potential allies who might be driven by economic necessity to make common cause with him but who are estranged by his attitude toward their cultural inheritances. Significantly communism has succeeded only in Russia, where the institutions and traditions of religion were particularly moribund. In the western world the uncom-

185

promising attitude toward religion is a source of confusion and political weakness and will continue to be so.

When Garibaldi initiated his romantic task of unifying Italy in the campaign against the Neapolitan tyranny in Sicily he found the priests and monks of Sicily ready to espouse his cause. The radical Mazzinian republicans in his ranks frowned upon this priestly support because they regarded all priests as reactionaries. But Garibaldi, with wiser statesmanship, welcomed any support that came to him and left it to the dogmatists in his ranks to speculate on the phenomenon of the revolutionary zeal among Sicilian priests. This is the kind of statesmanship which the radical movement in the western world sadly lacks.

A dogmatic collectivism in the philosophy of the proletarian and a too uncompromising attitude toward every form of individualism is another evidence of the blindness of vindictiveness and of the unconscious absolutizing of partial perspectives in radicalism. The proletarian worker is bound to be a collectivist and his collectivism is, in the main, a necessary instrument of social emancipation. The great centres of finance and industry must be taken out of private hands if modern civilization is to live. But the peasant cannot understand the collectivism of the proletarian. He will have to accept some of it even if he does not understand because his experience does not enable him to grasp the complete realities of a technical age. On the other hand his individualism has a measure of justification. He deals with a type of property which is not inevitably synonymous with power. It may merely present the individual with the possibility of performing his social function in society with a maximum degree of freedom. Large-scale collective farming may be more economical than the cultivation of small freeholds; but if it is, the economic advantages of collective farming rather than political pressure ought to be allowed to persuade the peasant to prefer one to the other.

In view of the fact that the whole world suffers from a glut of agricultural goods, greater efficiency in agriculture is not so important that it would not be wise to allow peasants even to sacrifice a degree of efficiency for the sake of preserving other values destroyed by collective farming. Dogmatic insistence on absolute collectivism for every type of social function merely reveals that the proletarian is driven by vindictive passions to condemn everything which resembles or reminds him of a social system which he intends to destroy. Its effect is to sacrifice life to consistency; and this effect is particularly dangerous to the proletarian cause in civilizations in which social complexities do not easily yield to the oversimplifications of a religious dogmatism. Specifically the inability of Marxian theory to deal adequately with the farm problem drives the peasants into the arms of the fascists in the entire western world.

The tendency of the lower middle classes and the farmers to fall into the hands of political reaction is, of course, due to other causes than the arrogant dogmatism of radicalism. It is partly due to the political incompetence and confusion of the agrarians and the poorer bourgeoisie. This political incompetence presents the protagonists of a new social order with a grave problem in strategy. If they fail to win the semi-neutral and the partially sympathetic classes to their cause they will prolong political reaction and augment its strength. This problem can be solved only if the disinherited industrial workers have some measure of appreciation for the unique social attitudes of classes related to but not identified with them.

If the proletarian movement does not come to terms more successfully with the middle class and the peasant problem than orthodox Marxism allows every western nation will fall into prolonged periods of fascist barbarism. A statesmanship which imagines that it can eliminate the confusion created by the presence of neutral and semi-neutral groups in a complex society by a fanatic fury which insists that there is no logical place for such groups in the scheme of things, succeeds merely in transmuting their neutrality and partial sympathy into pure antagonism.

That is what makes pure Marxism a peril to the cause of social radicalism in the entire western world.

If anything in heroic vehemence should be lost in tempering the spirit of vengeance by a charitable appreciation of forms of life and culture which are not strictly proletarian, the radical cause will find adequate compensation through the consequent enlargement of the basis of its political support. Here, as in other cases of history, a more profound moral insight may actually contribute to a prudent politics.

XIV

THE CONFLICT BETWEEN
CHRISTIANITY AND COMMUNISM

THE CONFLICT BETWEEN CHRISTIANITY AND COMMUNISM

IF communism may be regarded as the typical expression of the spiritual attitude of the proletarian rebels against a bourgeois civilization, it is significant that this attitude is informed by a peculiar combination of religion and irreligion. The reason communism has unfolded such a consistent animus against historic religion, particularly Christianity, is because it combines the hatred of one religion for another with the repulsion of irreligion for religion.

Communism is a religion in as far as it has a mythology which insists that human life and history have meaning. In the same sense the irreligious naturalism of bourgeois culture is religious. In both cases it is assumed that a scientific analysis of the course of history gives a valid picture of a sustained purpose and meaning in the confusion of incidents and events which comprise history. In both cases it is denied that this purpose has a conscious author or that there is any revelation of his intent in anything but the facts of history themselves. In as far as they are religions, both bourgeois naturalism and communism are non-theistic and naturalistic. For this reason they both disavow their religious character. But these disavowals are unconvincing to any one who realizes that it is quite impossible to establish a sense of meaning in history in scientific terms.

Science may give detailed accounts of the relation of isolated events to each other in various cause-effect series. But it cannot give a picture of the whole without introducing presuppositions which are not immediately apparent in the facts and can be found in them only after they have been suggested by the predisposition of the observer. The very fact that the history-pictures of bourgeois naturalism and proletarian communism are so completely different disproves their scientific pretensions. In the one case it is imagined that history moves gradually and by evolutionary inevitability toward an ethical goal. The world-view of bourgeois naturalism is optimistic. And the goal toward which history moves is an ethical ideal, characteristic of bourgeois life, the ideal of free co-operation, of a libertarian social order. The world-view of the proletarian is also optimistic. It is believed that a moral ideal will be completely realized in history. Significantly the ideal which is to be realized is one suggested by the needs and hopes of proletarian life, that of equal justice. But the proletarian world-view is not purely optimistic. There is a catastrophic note in it. The present social order will disintegrate before the ideal one can be established. A social system, which seems to those who profit from it to be essentially good and growing to perfection, appears to those who suffer from it to be constitutionally evil and tending toward catastrophe.

The actual contemporary facts of history seem to justify the more pessimistic proletarian philosophy of history much more than the purely optimistic bourgeois view and it is, by so much, more scientific. Nevertheless its confident faith, that good will grow out of disaster, belongs definitely to the category of mythology rather than science. Both the bourgeois idea of progress and the Marxian idea of salvation through catastrophe express a faith in the character of life and history which is religious rather than scientific because the mechanisms of history (the "what" and "how" of historic sequence) are subsumed under a purpose of history (the "why" of historic sequence); and this idea of purpose is in some sense or other the projection of human ideals upon cosmic reality. These allegedly irreligious world-views, no less than classical religion, are efforts to defeat pessimism by relating the conscious life of man to the great unconscious world. Like all religion, they deal with the problem of pessimism. They seek to defeat the pessimism and fear which naturally arise when conscious life surveys the world and finds consciousness dwarfed and rendered insignificant by the world's physical immensity and unconscious mechanism. They are, in other words, attempts to deal with the problem of evil; for the problem of evil is only superficially the problem of the suffering which sentient beings undergo in the world. Suffering is always bearable if it can be understood as a part of a process having a discernible end. What is insufferable to man is that his self-conscious existence should challenge the universe for a brief moment without being able to relate itself organically to it.

To understand the universe is to conquer it; but to understand it must mean in some sense to make it relevant to the human enterprise. Every world-view therefore, which finds the mechanisms of the cosmos either neutrally amenable or profoundly sympathetic to human ideals, is mythological and religious. It need not go as far as to discover a conscious author behind those mechanisms. Both bourgeois naturalism and communism fail to go to the length of finding conscious purpose in the universe because they emerge from a mechanistic civilization and a rationalistic culture. Such a civilization and such a culture atrophy the poetic imagination and therefore make it difficult to go beyond observable facts in conceiving a picture of the whole. A mechanistic civilization furthermore tends to dwarf and obscure consciousness

196

in human social relations and thereby makes it less available as a datum for a world picture.

Though the world-views of both bourgeois naturalism and proletarian communism are thus in the category of religious interpretations of life it is also true that they are irreligious. For a full-orbed religion not only interprets all events in history in terms of an ultimate meaning, but it also believes that this meaning and purpose transcend any immediate event or fact in historical reality. It is, in other words, dualistic and supernatural in its interpretation. This may be true even if it is ostensibly pantheistic, for in that case it may regard the natural world as something of a shadow or an illusion and distinguishes it from its "real" world which is the ideal world. The real basis for this dualism is ethical as well as philosophical. The meaning of life is conceived to be something which actual life only partially realizes or which it does not realize at all. Both the pessimism and the optimism of classical religion are, in other words, profounder than the attitudes of naturalistic religions. The idea that naturalistic religions are scientifically or philosophically more respectable than more dualistic religions merely proceeds from the temper of an age and has nothing to do with scientific or philosophical adequacy. It cannot have anything to do with scientific adequacy because science cannot concern itself with the ultimate character and meaning of reality. When it presumes to do so it has mistakenly drawn conclusions from detailed facts and descriptions which the facts have ostensibly yielded but which have been really supplied by assumptions and presuppositions of the scientist. Philosophical adequacy cannot be a final test of a world-view because every complete philosophy is a rationalized mythology which is judged by the inner consistency of its structure but which, because of the canon of consistency, cannot do justice to all the facts of paradoxical reality. The canons of logic and rationality are transcended when reason attempts to comprehend the final irrationality of things. Ultimate world-views therefore seem more or less rational to given ages and eras because they satisfy the temper of the day by doing justice to those facts which the age regards as particularly important.

The real difference between naturalistic monism and dualistic supernaturalism is derived from ethical feeling. If it is recognized or believed that the moral imagination conceives ideals for life which history in any immediate or even in any conceivable form is unable to realize a dualistic world-view will emerge. Thus classical religion with its various types of dualism grows out of the conflict of spirit and impulse in human life. All systems of high morality, whatever their differences, can be reduced to the demand that men shall affirm the life of others as much as they affirm their own. This demand of reason and conscience is in conflict with the natural egoistic impulse with which all life is endowed and which attempts the immediate and the exclusive preservation of the ego or the specific social organization, if need be at the expense of other life. It is this pressure of egoistic impulse in conflict with the moral imperative which is accurately described by Paul in the words: "There is a law in my members, warring against the law of my mind, and bringing me into captivity to the law of sin." A particularly pathetic aspect of this conflict in the human soul is that the very self-consciousness which makes moral criticism of natural impulse possible also endows egoistic impulse with particularly stubborn force.

Dualistic religions always emerge when human beings lose confidence in the possibility of life-as-impulse fulfilling all the demands of life-as-spirit. When, on the other hand, it is believed that spirit can bring the impulses of life completely under its dominion, morality becomes optimistic and the realization of the highest ethical ideal in history is hoped for. The naturalism of bourgeois culture is thus, at least partially, derived from the moral optimism of the bourgeois world.

The emergence of supernaturalism, which follows upon the discovery of the inertia and the persistence of the egoistic impulse in all nature including man, expresses itself in a twofold way. A source above the human is sought to explain the moral demands which transcend human capacities and therefore seem to have originated in superhuman sources ("For we know that the law is spiritual but I am carnal, sold under sin," Romans 7:14) ; and an order of reality is recognized in which a more than human perfection is achieved. ("Why callest thou me good? There is none good but one, that is, God, Matt. 19:17). There may be other sources of theism and supernaturalism in both primitive and modern psychic life but the experience of moral frustration is a perennial source of theistic belief and the guarantee of its regular emergence in human life.

Though it is never easy to relate the God of holiness and perfection, conceived by the religious imagination, with the actual facts of nature and history, an adequate mythology never fails to commit the rational absurdity of conceiving God as at once the pinnacle and the basis of reality, the goal toward which life is striving and the force by which it strives. It is forced to insist upon this connection lest, having solved the problem of life by finding its centre of meaning, it lose the solution by placing the centre so high above the realities of nature and history that these are lost again in chaos and mechanism. Christian theism has solved this problem by its conception of a transcendent-immanent God, a conception which can never be fully rationalized but which does justice both to the moral necessities of human life and to the actual facts of human experience; for experience constantly reveals harmonies, meanings and purposes which, by their very imperfection, suggest a perfection beyond them but which in spite of their imperfection contain elements of the perfection which transcends them.

The rational absurdity of the conception of a God who is at once immanent and transcendent arises only when the effort is made to transpose the original Jewish-Christian mythos of the creator and the creation into philosophical and scientific terms. In the creation myth God is transcendent in the sense that the potter is certainly above his clay and in a different category of existence. He is immanent in the sense that his creation is a revelation of his majesty and glory. Yet the very idea of immanence is a rational conception which falsifies the meaning of the mythos of the creator and the creation. Thus the very theology of a transcendent-immanent God reveals the difficulty of doing justice to the original meaning of a great mythos in rational terms.

Julien Benda, in a recent book, protests against the religious mythology which identifies the God of the goal and the God of the process: "It is clear that these two Gods . . . have nothing to do with each other. The God whom Marshal de Villars, rising in his stirrups

201

and pointing his drawn sword heavenwards, thanks on the evening of Denain, is one God; quite another is the God within whose bosom the author of the *Imitation of Christ*, in the corner of his cell, feels the nothingness of all human victories."[1] A very similar religious sentiment is at the basis of the insistence of modern German dialectic theology upon the transcendent God. But such protests cannot finally avail because in them religious pessimism becomes too consistent and renounces the significance and virtue of human history from the perspective of the very ideal through which life has been saved from chaos and meaninglessness.

The genius of classical religion is that it finds a basis for optimism after it has entertained the most thoroughgoing pessimism. In Buddhism the pessimism is so deep that the ultimate optimism remains somewhat lamed. In Christianity the triumph over pessimism is complete but, as the central place of the Cross in Christian thought symbolizes, it is not easy. In monistic optimistic world-views rational man is conceived as triumphing over the chaos of nature or of history. In the classical religious world-view man himself is conceived as a source of chaos. His egoistic impulses are properly recognized as perennial sources of social chaos, and no complete emancipation from

[1] Julien Benda, *Essai d'un discours, cohérent sur les rapports de Dieu et du monde.*

the confusion and self-destruction of conflicting egoisms is expected in mundane history. Such emancipation is expected only above history (in the Greek view) or at the end of history (according to Hebrew mythology).

Judged by the criteria of optimism and pessimism the difference between bourgeois naturalism, communism and classical Christianity is that the first is purely optimistic because it finds ethical values completely immanent in the processes of nature and history. Communism is partially pessimistic because it finds the historical process of the moment running counter to its socio-moral ideal. But it is ultimately optimistic because it believes an organization of society possible in which the chaos of egoistic impulse will be fully overcome. This optimism is more closely related to Christian theism than liberal naturalism because it believes that something more than purely rational ethical activity contributes to the victory of the good. It believes for instance that there is a logic in history which makes for the self-destruction of evil (the destruction of capitalistic injustice through its own inherent contradictions).

The optimism of Christianity is quite different from either of these because its pessimism is profounder. This judgment does not, of course, hold for liberal Christianity because it is based upon an ethical optimism which makes it more akin to modern naturalism than to classical religion. Its optimistic view of human nature destroys the ethical and psychological basis for its supernatural theism. That is why its theism disintegrates into a naturalistic pantheism however bravely or foolishly it may seek to hide it. Liberal Christianity always imagines that it has adjusted the affirmations of classical religion to the "discoveries of modern science." But modern science has comparatively little to do with its orientation. The real basis for it is its faith in the goodness of human nature or confidence in the possibility of realizing the ethical ideals in the world of history which are projected by the highest moral imagination of man. In the more classical version of the Christian religion man remains a sinner in spite of all moral achievements. In other words it is recognized that from an absolute perspective every moral achievement reveals an alloy of egoistic impulse. The proof that something more than morbid perfectionism is involved in this insistence of classical religion is given by the fact that every co-operative achievement in human history actually has the possibilities of providing collective egoism with wider and more destructive forms of expression.

The peril of classical religion is that its ultimate optimism tends to be supramoral because it has emerged from a pessimism so profound as to question the moral significance of every moral achievement. That is why any social religion, which is intent upon the achievement of relative goals of social righteousness in history, must come in conflict with those forms of classical religion in which supramoral and ultramundane optimism has been stressed to such a degree as to rob the historical struggle for the realization of the ideal of its significance.

THE POLITICAL REALISM OF
CHRISTIAN ORTHODOXY

THE POLITICAL REALISM OF
CHRISTIAN ORTHODOXY

THE test of the realism of a moral or religious world-view is its attitude toward politics because in that attitude it reveals its understanding of the persistence and inertia of collective egoism against the aspirations and demands of the spirit. A religious world-view may pessimistically regard the world of politics as the nemesis of the moral ideal, as is the tendency in Christian orthodoxy; or it may look upon political power as the instrument of the moral ideal without recognizing that power as an instrument of an ideal may easily corrupt the ideal, as in communism; or it may fail to make any distinction between the field of morals and politics and fondly imagine that moral ideals are inevitably applied to the political world, once they are generally accepted, as in liberalism.

Both liberalism and radicalism have a touch of romanticism which blinds them to the Janus-faced character of political life and obscures the fact that man's collective life and corporate actions provide both a reservoir into which the individual may pour his altruistic purposes and a spring for the stream of dark and turgid passions which outrage the finer sensibilities of the human spirit. Radicalism is more realistic than liberalism in gauging the social forces of a contemporary situation and recognizing that a new social order must emerge out of a conflict of interest and impulse as much as from a conquest of impulse by reason; but it is no more realistic than liberalism in its final analysis of the social problem because it believes in the possibility of establishing a social order in which the conflict of interest and impulse can be finally and completely abolished.

In contrast to this romantic utopianism the virtue of Christianity from the beginning has been that it has had no illusions about the world of politics. Its moral demands were absolute; and judged by these absolute criteria the inequalities and injustices, the conflicts and the coercive measures of the political world seemed to it to be the most vivid symbols of the sinfulness of man. Classical Christianity also has its visions of the future, akin to romantic utopianism. But in these visions it is always a redeemed humanity which established the ideal society. Even if it is established on earth, as in the vision of the prophets and Jesus, it will be a society governed by pure spirit. In such a society there will be "neither marriage nor giving in marriage," no impulses of the flesh, in short.

This fact may make Christian eschatology irrelevant to every political ethic which must deal with the vexing problem of bringing inner and social checks upon collective impulse; but it does save it from the illusions of secular utopianism.

In the teachings of Jesus the love ideal is stated unqualifiedly and loyalty to it is demanded without a suggestion of those compromises which political realities seem to make inevitable. Men are to love their neighbors as themselves, they are not to resist evil, not to resent injustice, not to desire concrete and obvious rewards, in short not to assert the ego against the life around it. The rigor of this ethic is saved from the pessimistic conclusion of Buddhistic ethics about the evil nature of all life and desire by the paradox of discovering self-fulfillment and self-realization as a legitimate, though unintended, consequence of self-abnegation. Thus life is affirmed though the virtue of the ego's impulse to affirm his own life is denied.

This ethical paradox, so basic to the teachings of Jesus, is completely justified by the facts of life and history. It is really true that the threat of death and extinction, or at least of incomplete self-realization, is involved in all natural impulses of survival and all narrow attempts at self-realization. The life of each individual and group is organic to the whole and the thrust of the part against the whole destroys the organic harmony which sustains each part. It must not be assumed however that the rational realization of this fact will ever completely check the inordinate impulses toward survival and fulfillment with which men are endowed. Human history must remain a perpetual conflict between conscience and nature; and the forces of nature are so powerful in it that complete devotion to the ethical principle would lead to annihilation in any immediate instant.

The ethical ideal grants its uncompromising devotees the promised self-fulfillment only if self-fulfillment is thought of in completely spiritual terms, as for instance the immortality of fame and influence or the "rewards in the resurrection of the just" in the mythology of Jesus. This is true in individual life. It is doubly true in the relation of human groups, in which the forces of nature, blind impulse and passion, are more powerful than in the life of individuals. For this reason the effort to reduce the ethic of Jesus to a prudential ethic, to a utilitarian calculation of the best way of achieving self-realization in ordinary history must always fail. If Jesus ever had a faith in the possibility of making the love ideal progressively applicable to the present world (a faith comparable to that of liberal Protestantism), it belonged to the early days of his ministry and was transmuted into a catastrophic hope as his own cross became imminent.

There are nevertheless real possibilities of extending the principle of love in historic life. The teachings of Jesus have thus given inspiration to both the optimists and the pessimists. To the one they have presented a moral goal possible of progressive achievement. To the others they have become the foundation for a religion which revealed the contrast between God and man, between the ideal toward which men are drawn and the inertia of nature which frustrates the attainment of the highest ideal.

The Christian religion is thus an ethical religion in which the optimism, necessary for the ethical enterprise, and the pessimism, consequent upon profound religious insights, never achieve a perfect equilibrium or harmony. On the whole, however, the religious note triumphed over the purely ethical one. The purely ethical note never gained the ascendency in classical Christianity, either primitive, mediæval or protestant. It did triumph in modern liberal Protestantism. Its victory there was significantly due to influence of eighteenth-century rationalism and nineteenth-century liberálism and not to elements in Christianity itself. In classical Christianity the contrast between the moral ideal and the facts of history is too sharp to allow for a pure ethical optimism. Its insistence upon the transcendence of God and the fact of original sin is an authentic mythological expression of its understanding for the perennial con-

213

flict between the moral ideal and the impulses of nature.

Naturally this pessimistic note in Christianity expresses itself most unqualifiedly in its attitude toward politics; because it is in the realities of politics and the facts of collective human behavior that the inertia of nature against the impulses of the spirit is most apparent. Jesus made no concessions to the necessities of political life. He counselled acquiescence toward the political *status quo* ("Render unto Cæsar the things that are Cæsar's") and refused to interfere in questions of economic justice ("Who hath made me a divider over you?"). His indifference toward politics cannot, however, be interpreted in terms of individualistic perfectionism. The kingdom of God of which he spoke was a social conception. True to his Jewish heritage he believed that it would be established upon earth. The note of supraworldliness, introduced into Christianity by Greek thought, was foreign to him. In respect to his emphasis upon a goal to be realized in the mundane world he was closer to the this-worldly hopes of liberalism and communism than the otherworldliness of orthodox Christianity. But his thought is to be distinguished from modern hopes for an ideal social order by the apocalyptic note in it. He did not believe that man had the resources to establish an ideal society. That would come only through the

214

grace of God. His followers could prepare for it by
contrition and prayer but not by any premature effort to establish justice through coercion. He did
not counsel resistance to Roman oppression and called
attention to the self-defeating character of violence.
His indifference toward the moral problem of politics did not, however, relax the moral tension upon social problems. The absolute moral ideal for political
society was maintained by his apocalyptic hope.

This same hope made it possible for the early
church to insist on an absolute ethic without facing
the responsibilities of the political problem. Not until the hope of the second coming of the Saviour vanished and the church had grown from a politically ir-
responsible sect to a community embracing an empire did it come to terms with the political problem.
When it did so its doctrine of the fall of man provided it with a basis for the compromises with an absolute moral ideal demanded by the political realities. According to the absolute ideal, man was intended to live in perfect love and complete equality
with his fellowmen. But his fall into sin made this
impossible and created a situation in which the evil
lusts of men needed to be checked by the coercion of
governments, the restrictions of property and even
the inequalities of slavery. The problems of economics and politics were to be regulated by the requirements of "natural law" rather than the absolute

ideal of love, a conception which Christianity borrowed from Stoicism. The requirements of the natural law were, broadly speaking, the demands of *justice* (though never equalitarian justice) and they were assumed to have been written into all human hearts by God. In as far as they were not voluntarily obeyed (and the prevalence of sin would make infractions inevitable) they were to be enforced by governments. Government had, in fact, been expressly instituted by God for this purpose. Here the orthodox church from the earliest day to the present has leaned heavily on the words of Paul. "There is no power but of God; the powers that be are ordained of God."

If one were to reconstruct this general philosophy of politics in non-mythological terms it might be put in the following words: The highest moral ideal for human life, the ideal of love can neither be renounced nor completely realized. Its imperative and convincing reality proves that human life has its source and its goal above and beyond the frustrations and hindrances of the world of nature in which man lives. In this world the inordinate egoism of individuals and groups constantly threatens life with self-destruction through anarchy. Since obedience to the absolute demands of love is impossible to natural man he must be restrained by an ideal less rigorous but nevertheless effective in preventing the strong from devouring the weak and from living in the anarchy of constant conflict. The law of justice is such an ideal. It is the moral ideal in a more negative form than the ideal of love. It demands not that the interests of the neighbor be affirmed but that interests of the self be restricted so that they will not infringe upon those of the neighbor. Furthermore it sanctions the coercive force of governments to restrain those who will not voluntarily abide by the rule of rational justice.

Such a brief statement of the orthodox conception of the relation of the gospel ideal to the fall and the natural law hardly does justice to all the various elaborations of the basic ideas developed through the ages. But it suffices to prove that the total conception is informed by a realism which does justice to more facts of both morals and politics than most modern moral and political theories. Yet it presents serious difficulties. They arise partly from the inexactness of mythological thinking. Such thought is usually more profound in its grasp of the total realities of the human situation than exact scientific thinking. But it is usually wanting in precise distinctions.

This lack of precision is evidenced by the fact that Christian orthodoxy in one moment pessimistically consigns the world of politics to the world of nature unredeemed and unredeemable. In the next moment it sanctifies the institutions which have brought relative order into its chaos, and the relative justice which they have achieved, into ordinances of God. The moral possibilities in political life are gravely imperilled in each instance.

The deleterious effect of both the pessimism and the religious sanctification of social injustice in Christian thought is clearly revealed in its attitude toward slavery. With the Stoics, Christianity recognized equality as the ideal for all human relations. But the fall of man into sin made this ideal impossible of realization. It became therefore a religious rather than an ethical ideal. All men were to be regarded as equal in the sight of God and, within limits, in the religious community. The fact that this religious ideal of equality did prompt many Christians to grant manumission to their slaves proves that it was not without ethical potency. But on the whole slavery was accepted as both a punishment and remedy for sin. It regularized and thereby checked the evil lusts of men. The idea that slavery was a punishment for sin naturally tempted to the conclusion that it was the sin of the slave which was being punished. This implication is indeed made explicit in the thought of both Saint Ambrose and Saint Isidore of Seville and it is not foreign to the thought of Saint Augustine.[1] If it was obvious in an individual instance that the slave

[1] *Cf.* R. W. Carlyle, *A History of Medieval Political Theory in the West,* Vol. I, p. 118.

was better than his master he was nevertheless counselled to obedience in conformity with the Christian
ideal of non-resistance and in accordance with explicit scriptural instructions.[2] The injunction to accept social inequality both as a punishment for sin
and as an opportunity to display Christian virtue
(the virtue of patience and non-resistance) manages
to combine all the dangers of an absolute ethic and a
sanctifying religion. The religion declares social evil
to be divinely ordained and the pure ethic makes resistance to it morally inadmissible. The result is
moral confusion which borders on moral perversity.
Nor is the confusion confined to the mediæval church.
Luther's attitude toward the rebellious peasants in the
sixteenth century is prompted by exactly the same
elements in Christian doctrine.[3]

The Christian attitude toward government reveals
the same tendency to combine pessimistic realism with
regard to the evils of government with a religious
justification of those evils. The perspective of the
pure love ethic makes the Christian church conscious
of brutal realities of politics. The love ideal implies
uncoerced co-operation: but governments are by their
nature coercive. Yet their power is divinely ordained
and the coercion which they use is a requisite of social

[2] Cf. I Peter 2:18-20 and Eph. 6:5.
[3] Cf. Luther's *Werke Gesammtausgabe* (Weimar), Vol. 18, pp.
300-75.

cohesion and a guarantee against graver injustice in a sinful world.

Sometimes the Christian pessimism has driven theologians to question the divine ordinance of government. Thus, for instance, Gregory VII declares: "Who does not know that kings and rulers had their beginning in men inspired by the devil, the prince of the world, to turn from God and presume in the blindness of their lusts and their intolerable arrogance to bear their rule over men, *their equals*, through pride, violence, fraud, bloodshed and almost every known crime?"[4] Augustine's realism tempts him to similar descriptions of the evils of the state, equally at variance with the more accepted doctrine of the state as a divine ordinance. This doctrine, however, first developed by Irenæus and Justin Martyr in the second century, has varied little to the present day. Government is divinely ordained and morally justified because a sinful world would, without the restraints of the state, be reduced to anarchy by its evil lusts.

Thus Christian thought may represent a realistic and unavoidable compromise with the necessities of political life and therefore deserves preference over the efforts of less realistic moderns, inside and outside of the church, to force a pure ethical ideal into

4 Quoted by C. H. McIlwain, *The Growth of Political Thought in the West,* p. 207.

the stubborn inertia of the political order. But the weakness of the orthodox Christian position is that its pessimism and its religious sanctification of the political order discourage the ambition of a high morality to correct the abuses of the political order and to fashion a political organization which would be least likely to result in anarchy or to tolerate tyranny.

The fact that individual states, though they may be the very basis of order for their own nation, have a will-to-power which makes for anarchy between nations was never considered by the church, except in as far as it gave mediæval theologians an opportunity to assert the supremacy of the church over the state. What is even more important, no sound principle of political change emerges anywhere in Christian thought. Aquinas distinguishes between necessary coercion and tyranny and he even suggests that governments have only delegated power. But his thought offers criteria for the moral criticism of governments rather than principles of political resistance to their inordinate exactions.

Even when political resistance is allowed, as in the thought of Chrysostom or Abelard, the right to resistance is confined to the person of an evil ruler and not permitted against the government which he incarnates.[5] The prevailing note in Christian ortho-

[5] Abelard's words are: "It is one thing to resist the tyranny of an evil ruler; it is another to resist his just power which he has from God." Quoted by McIlwain, *op. cit.*, p. 153.

doxy, both Protestant and Catholic, is one which discourages resistance to government and which usually implies not only that government as such but that monarchial government is divinely ordained. Not infrequently patience with unjust governments is enjoined for the same reasons which are advanced for the acceptance of slavery. It is only in Calvinism, particularly in Scotch and Dutch Calvinism, that the Christian conception of natural law is clearly developed in terms which justify resistance not only to individual tyrants but against an established type of political organization.

These weaknesses of the political theories of Christian orthodoxy are not simply to be ascribed to the intellectual immaturity of the church in other ages. They are partly derived from difficulties which a profound religion necessarily faces when it deals with political problems. A pure spirituality, expressed in individual terms, easily leads to counsels of acquiescence in political injustice; and a conventional piety tends to sanctify established political forms. Thus the force of both spirituality and piety in religion may easily combine to create moral confusion in politics.

The pessimistic assumption of classical religion that no political order can fully incarnate the highest ideal is the natural consequence of the transcendent perspective of high religion. If the perils of a morbid perfectionism and of a concomitant socio-moral defeatism are inherent in it, it remains nevertheless a necessary moral resource. It prevents individuals and groups from indulging in the proud illusion that any of their social purposes are completely free of egoism. Through the insights of high religion the alloy of selfishness in every human enterprise is discovered and the perils of anarchy and tyranny are recognized in every social achievement. Naturally religion cannot perform the task of offering such insights without running the danger of moral defeatism. When life is viewed from a transcendent perspective it becomes plausible to regard the distinctions between the "nicely calculated less and more" of political justice as insignificant, since both the evil and the good fall short of the ideal set by the purest conscience.

During a recent visit of a bishop of the Russian church to America a group of Russian Czarist émigrés heckled the leader of their church because of his supposed sympathies with communism. The bishop explained that Christianity was not interested in political systems or their comparative merits but only in preaching salvation to "sinful" men in any political system. He was asked whether he prayed for the soul of the Czar and replied in the affirmative, whereupon a critic cried in derision, "Do you pray for Stalin too," and the bishop replied quietly: "Yes, I pray for the soul of the Czar and for Stalin and for every sinner including myself." This incident rather aptly illustrates classical Christianity's preoccupation with the problem of sin in general. It seems to justify the critical vigilance which communism or any other great social passion must preserve against a perspective in religion which reduces all social and moral striving to a single category of "sinfulness" and makes ethical distinctions on the historical level impossible.

It is important to remember however that the animus of communism against Christianity is derived not only from a social passion which finds religious complacency dangerous but also from an ethical utopianism which is too superficial to plumb the depths of evil illumined by a profound religion. Joseph Wood Krutch reports the greatest of Russian cinema directors as declaring: "My aim is to destroy the moving picture." Pressed for an explanation of this self-devouring artistic ambition Eisenstein said: "There are two kinds of art, bourgeois art and proletarian art. The first is an effort to compensate for unsatisfied desire. The second is preparation for social change. Now in the perfect state there will be no bourgeois art because there will be no unsatisfied desire. There will also be no proletarian art because there will be no further necessity for social change. Therefore since I am working for the perfect state I

am also working to destroy the moving picture."[6] All
communist utopians would not draw as consistent conclusions from their premises as does Eisenstein, but
the Russian moving picture director's words taken in
conjunction with the doctrine of grace of the Russian bishop illustrate rather tellingly how the battle
between Christianity and communism is a battle between a religion which tends to lose its moral force
by a too transcendent perspective and a moral passion which loses its religious profundity by superficial confidence in the establishment of some ethical
absolute in history. Here, as so frequently in history, two historic life-views become completely incompatible because the truth neglected by the one is
made the basis of error by the other. Probably each
side, having half the truth, protests against the other
side the more vehemently because it dimly suspects
that the error of the foe is a suppressed portion of its
truth.

[6] Joseph Wood Krutch, "Literature and Utopia," *The Nation*,
Oct. 18, 1933, p. 442.

XVI

A RADICAL POLITICAL THEORY

XVI

A RADICAL POLITICAL
THEORY

AN adequate approach to the social and moral problem must include a political policy which will bring the most effective social check upon conflicting egoistic impulses in society; a moral idealism which will exploit every available resource of altruistic impulse and reason to extend life from selfish to social ends; and a religious world-view which will do justice to the ideals of the spirit which reach beyond the possibilities of historic achievement and thereby challenge every concrete attainment with the vision of the unattained.

The modern world-view in its sober and prudential rationality fails to comprehend the total dimensions of human life. It does not take sufficient account either of the stubborn impulses which operate below the level of reason and express themselves particularly in those relations with which an adequate politics must deal, or with the ideals of pure love and self-sacrifice which burst the bounds of the canons of prudential morality and reveal the human spirit in its final protest against the impulses of nature. The modern view considers only what life reveals in the conventional and tame relations in which reason has checked and extended natural impulses. It fails to see the higher and lower dimensions where life is more purely nature and more purely spirit. An adequate world-view must do justice to life on all three levels. This can only be done by a radical political theory, a theory in morals which allows for both the prudence of liberalism and the disinterestedness of radical religion; and finally an idea of "grace" as found only in classical religion.

A political policy which deals effectively with the problem of life-as-impulse, and knows how to gain a rough justice and a minimal harmony from the chaos of human passions, must be radical. It must be able to discount the usual rational and moral justifications for a given system of justice and injustice and must inquire what forces of nature, accidents of history, advantages of birth and caprices of life established the particular kind of disproportion of power out of which the justices and injustices of that social system have emerged. It must be radical not only in the realistic nature of its analysis but in its willingness to challenge the injustice of a given social system by setting power against power until a more balanced equilibrium of power is achieved. Radical policy inevitably grows out of a radical theory which recognizes that human life is never completely moral and that minimum justice therefore depends upon the ability of society to level the centres of excessive power which are the bases of injustice.

Such a radicalism distinguishes itself both from the orthodox Christian approach to politics and from the modern liberal moral approach. The Christian religious approach is more realistic than the modern liberal approach, as we have seen, but it is defective because it regards any given political and social order as divinely ordained. This orthodox position is derived from a too unqualified pessimism. It is grateful for any social order whatsoever and fears to disturb it lest anarchy should result. It proceeds furthermore from an uncritical piety which too readily transfigures the forces of nature, which have established a given political order, into instruments of God. It is, in other words, closely related to the attitudes of primitive society toward the customs which regulated its life. Any custom whatever, though it may have been established by a caprice of history, was given a rigid inflexibility by primitive society because religious sanctions absolutized it and because lack of imagination and fear of anarchy made an established social check upon the anarchy of impulse seem to be the only possible alternative to chaos.

The sentiments of piety are always dangerous when dealing with social facts because they so easily give a religious aura to social conditions created by purely natural or even brutal forces. A king who reaches his throne by killing his brother is immediately invested with religious sanctity because he represents "powers ordained of God." A strong man, whether he be a military or financial oligarch, arrogates political power to himself and the piety of the community transmutes his position into a divine ordinance. Political facts must be analyzed by a critical, sophisticated, not to say cynical, intelligence.

A radical political theory must distinguish itself as sharply from moral sentimentality as from religious piety. Modern liberalism imagines itself much more sophisticated than religious piety. But it results in equally dangerous illusions. It inclines to attribute injustice to ignorance and it therefore encourages the victims of injustice to wait until it has converted their oppressors from selfishness to unselfishness. It does not realize that the intelligence and the moral idealism of the average man are never able to accomplish more than the mitigation of the injustices of a given disproportion of power. Moral sentiment is an oil which reduces the frictions of a given system of social relationships but it changes the relationships only in the rarest instances. It is like the tides of the sea which take off the edges of the pebbles on the beach but leave the cliffs standing.

Moral idealism may persuade slave-owners to be

kind to their slaves but it has prompted only a few slave-owners to free their serfs. Even the absolute love ideal of the early Christian community quickly sloughed off the communistic implications inherent in its absolutism and degenerated into a counsel of philanthropy. The ideal of philanthropy encourages those who have more than they need to be generous with those who have too little. But there are only very rare instances in the history of philanthropy in which generosity became so heedless as to reduce the benefactor to the level of power and privilege of his beneficiaries. The fact that there are a few such cases proves that rare individuals do occasionally rise above the level of common egoism. The fact that the cases are rare proves that political strategy must not take too much account of them.

The intelligence of even very sensitive individuals is usually not pure enough to make an absolutely objective estimate of the claims which other lives make upon the common goods of society in competition with the self. The ideals of justice which animate those who have the power to give and to withhold privilege are therefore never equal to the canons of an abstract justice. Thus a generous housewife may increase the wages of a charwoman or laundress because she has discovered that her servant is the sole support of a family of four children. But she will hardly engage in disquieting speculations about the causes of the disproportion in power and privilege which permit her, perhaps a woman with one child, to coerce a mother of four children into her service. If she engaged in such speculations she might discover that there are no moral or rational justifications for the economic power which she wields over the other woman. It may be due to accidents of history, to fortunes of birth or to endowments of beauty and charm. She may have been able to capture a husband in a lucrative and safe position while the other woman was fated to an early widowhood because she married, let us say, a coal miner. The servant may be more intelligent than her mistress and her children may have a moral right to a greater share of society's privileges of leisure, education and security than the mistress's one child. All this has nothing to do with the immediate situation however. For superior economic power enables the one woman to hire the other. And the most sensitive conscience will hardly persuade her to go further than to be more than ordinarily generous with her servant. That may be taken as a parable of the general effect of moral sentiment upon the established social relations. It explains why a measure of hypocrisy attaches to all but the purest moral pretensions and also why the political task of dealing with the roots of social injustice must precede the moral task of building imaginative justice upon the foundations of the rough justice of politics. If the moral task precedes or displaces the political one it leads to moral confusions as great as the illusions of piety in politics.

In dealing with the political task which confronts every society and particularly a society, such as the contemporary one, in which social injustice has reached proportions which threaten social stablility, the problem is to prevent or to destroy the accumulation of social power and to bring the irreducible minimum under the strongest possible social check. In modern society this means that economic power must be dealt with rigorously because it is the most significant power. In the present situation it is obvious that anything which qualifies or circumscribes the power of economic ownership will ultimately make for justice. We have previously noted that there is a tendency in history that social injustice provides the means of its own undoing and this tendency is particularly apparent in the present moment of social disintegration. There is furthermore the possibility that skill in operating the modern technical productive process may naturally become a source of more significant social power than the ownership of the instruments of that process. We are therefore living in a moment of history in which power is being equalized.

But history does not move automatically and

whether these tendencies will rapidly make for greater justice in society depends to a considerable degree upon the number of people who understand the logic which is working itself out in modern history and who are willing to affirm rather than defy it. If it is defied the next decades may have to witness indescribable tortures before a new and more stable society is built. Since those who hold most power and privilege in society are bound to attempt defiance there is no possibility of escaping a very considerable social conflict and confusion. But modern society has large classes who neither suffer from acute injustice nor benefit from it to a great degree. They are, to some extent, neutral elements in the situation. Yet they cannot remain neutral when the final hour of crisis and decision comes. These are the very classes which have been most confused by religious and moral illusions in the past. If they could gain a clearer view of the political realities they might greatly modify the social distress and confusion through which the coming generations must pass.

The political realism which is demanded of these classes does not, as is usually assumed, preclude the possibilities of genuine moral idealism. To understand history-as-nature does not mean that the human spirit need to capitulate prematurely to the impulses which express themselves in it. The fact is that the highest type of disinterestedness is necessary if those who are not driven by an immediate pressure of interest are to help guide the processes of history which are determined to a large degree by conflicting interests. No new society can be built either without the assertion of interest on the part of those who have been defrauded in an old society or without the disinterested affirmation of the interests of the disinherited on the part of some who have not been disinherited. If the force contributed by the relatively disinterested is lacking, society may sink into an anarchy of unresolved conflicts of interest.

Every modern society contains a goodly portion of "moral idealists" who are genuinely interested in a more perfect social justice. They have been prevented from making any great contribution to their desired goal partly by the moral scruples derived from the illusions of liberalism and partly by remnants of class pride and class fear. Their relative security in an established society tempts them to regard a change in the social system with apprehension and their modest property interests prompt them to be critical toward the radical goal of social ownership. In other words prejudices arising from egoistic impulses combine with honest moral scruples in determining their political attitudes. Increased economic pressure in a decaying social system will serve to dissipate some of these prejudices. But they must be partly dispelled by a rational appreciation of the inevitability and desirability of the goal of social ownership.

If modern society moves with inexorable logic toward collectivism that does not mean that all property will be as rigorously collectivized as it has been in Russia, nor that socialization will solve all political and moral problems. It means only that the disproportion of economic power, inherent in the private ownership of social processes, is the main cause of modern injustice and that this particular cause will therefore be eliminated or mitigated by social ownership. In moving toward this goal modern society is merely reappropriating the experience of primitive society. In the hunting and pastoral periods of civilization there was a large measure of common ownership because it was incompatible with the interest of the whole society that resources and instruments which all required should be privately owned. Thus streams for fishing, hunting grounds, frequently weapons of the hunt and finally grazing lands were owned in common.

The agricultural period introduced private ownership and, though it led to the evils of landlordism, it is nevertheless true that private ownership is still more compatible with justice in the field of agriculture than in any other field. Modern technology, however, has made the traditions of private ownership inapplicable to industrial society. It has created vast technical processes upon which a whole society depends and which are operated by the greater portion of the workers of society. It is obvious therefore that the granting of peculiar rights of ownership in these instruments of production to a special class of owners is to invite those injustices which always result from centralization of power.

Thus modern society is forced by the conditions introduced by the machine to return to social ideals once held by early society. The more the intelligent portions of a community recognize this development as both inevitable and desirable the quicker will be the period of transition in which society now lives and the more certainly will the dangers of barbarism be avoided.

XVII

THE BALANCE OF POWER IN POLITICS

XVII

THE BALANCE OF POWER
IN POLITICS

To concede that justice in political relations depends upon a balance of power is to admit that even the most imaginative political policy will fail to achieve perfect justice. A balance of power implies a conflict of wills and contest of interests in which injustice is prevented because contending forces are fairly evenly matched. Such a procedure does not remove the root of conflict which is to be found in the corporate egoism of contending groups. As long as the character and nature of man is not changed into something now quite unknown in human history, neither a new and more perfect social pedagogy nor a more perfect social organization will be able to eliminate all possibilities of injustice and conflict in human society.

There is obviously no guarantee of stability in any social harmony which rests upon a precarious balance of power. A fortuitous change in weights may easily upset the balance. A society which establishes an economic equilibrium through social ownership may thus create a new disproportion of power through the necessity of strengthening the political force which holds economic life in check. The new and stronger centres of political power will be new occasions for and temptations to injustice. Temptations to the unjust use of power can always be mitigated by bringing every centre of significant power under social control and surveillance. The need of such control makes the instruments of democracy, whatever their limitations, a perennial necessity in any society. Oligarchs will violate the principles of justice to some degree even when a democratic check is placed upon their power. Without such a check every oligarchy becomes tyrannical. The communist faith that communist oligarchs will not make selfish use of their power belongs in the same category of illusions which aristocracies of the past have nourished. They also believed that it was the business of the wise man to rule because he governed unselfishly and that they were the wise men. But aristocracies, whether priestly or military, have always been corrupted in the end by the poison of power, whatever may have been the moral pretensions or ideals with which they began.

A difference must be made between oligarchs who gloried in inequality and those who consciously and sincerely believe in equality. But the concession allowed must not be too generous. When the first fine careless rapture of a revolutionary and creative period of history is dissipated even oligarchs who consciously believe in equality may introduce inordinate privilege and power into society while they continue to pay lip service to the equalitarian ideal. And such are the complexities of a technical civilization that a perfectly valid justification will be found for every divergence from the equalitarian principle introduced, whether it be modest or inordinate.

An equilibrium of power may not only become unstable by the fortuitous or necessary creation of new disproportions of power but it may be destroyed by the underlying conflict of interest which is basic to it. Every balance of power and every equilibrium of social forces is a potential chaos which has been coaxed into a momentary cosmos. The chaos will occasionally erupt. Thus for instance it is becoming increasingly clear that Russian communism has not achieved a perfect identity and mutuality of interest between the peasants and the industrial workers. There is not even a perfect equilibrium of power between them, the industrial workers having the superior political power. There is no reason why the peasants might not in a future day pit their potentially superior economic power against the superior political power of the communist apparatus and create a new social conflict. Even if no overt conflict should take place there will be political conflicts between peasants and workers for ages to come in Russia and probably in every other modern nation. The conflict will be inevitable because industrial workers need socialization with greater urgency than the peasants.

The peace of nations is another example of precarious order on the edge of disorder. The peace of Europe before the World War rested upon a balance of power. It was destroyed by the mutual fears and animosities created by the tensions of such a balance. The peace of Europe since the war depends not upon a balance but upon a disproportion of power. It is secured by the supremacy of French arms. It is certain therefore that the present peace is more unstable than the last one.

One method of mitigating the perils of the balance of power is to guarantee its equilibrium by the force of the total society which encloses the contestants in any particular contest of wills and competition of interest. Such a society, whether it be a league of nations disciplining the nations or a national society arbitrating between individuals, actually does prevent covert conflicts from issuing into overt violence. Sometimes it may even function to correct injustice. But no society can permanently guarantee either peace or justice. It cannot guarantee justice because the organs of every society must be manipulated by some person, class or nation which is less than the whole and which will lack both the intelligence and will to comprehend the needs of the whole. It cannot guarantee peace because it is unable to revise the imperfect justice of any given society and it therefore invites the victims of injustice to resent the oppressions from which they suffer and "to take the law into their own hands." They do not do this until injustice becomes unbearable and human society therefore enjoys long periods of freedom from open hostilities, at least within the borders of particular national units.

The inability of the League of Nations to make any thorough revision of the injustices of the Treaty of Versailles was a perfect proof that a society of nations, at least in the present stage of human development, cannot preserve the peace. For if an unjust peace cannot be revised that proves that reason and conscience are not powerful enough to correct the injustices created by victorious power and vindictive passion. Their inability to do this means that the injustices will be corrected (and probably new ones created) by the vehement resentments of those who suffer from injustice. That is why a new war in Europe is only a matter of years.

It is clearly impossible to establish an ideal social harmony either within nations or between nations. The world of politics remains a "world of sin." Not because any given political strategy is inadequate but because there is no perfect restraint either moral or social for egoistic impulse, particularly not for the corporate egoism of social groups. Political strategy is therefore as definitely limited in its effectiveness as any purely rational or religious approach to the social problem. A recognition of these limits saves the student of politics from romantic over-beliefs. It will discourage only those who have not looked deeply into the realities of social life. The realists who have recognized the limits of politics in the establishment of justice will be encouraged to supplement pure politics with resources of reason and imagination in the hope of perfecting the rough justice of the political order with the refinements of rational justice and imaginative altruism.

XVIII

THE LIBERAL SPIRIT IN MORALS

THE LIBERAL SPIRIT
IN MORALS

RADICALISM as a method of observation brushes the moral pretensions and cultural elaborations of a given civilization aside to discover what kind of power-relations is to be found at the foundation of the social structure. Radicalism as a method of action seeks to level centres of power in the interest of justice. The radical is therefore necessary in every society but he is particularly needed in an era in which old social forms are disintegrating and new ones are emerging. Yet the radical cannot build or preserve a society unaided.

Radicalism is so intent upon bringing the covert conflicts in society into the open and upon discounting the ethical pretensions of power-politics that its eye is not accustomed to recognize and to appreciate the elements of mutual accord which actually develop in every social situation. If the liberal spirit is beset by the sin of hypocrisy because it inclines to provide moral refinements for essential unmoral relations, the besetting sin of a consistent radicalism is cruelty, because it fails to appreciate the motives of honest sympathy and justice which manifest themselves in any society. The pure radical has difficulty in coming to terms with his foe short of the foe's annihilation and in organizing a society by other than tyrannical means. The liberal spirit therefore remains a needed resource in building and preserving a community. The virtues of the liberal spirit are difficult to appreciate in a period in which the most penetrating intellects are still in full flight from the illusions and deceptions of liberalism. But ultimately it will be realized again that even a classless society, in which distinctions based upon privilege and property have been eliminated, will require the accommodations of interest to interest and right to right in which the liberal spirit is peculiarly adept. The extension of rational justice and the encouragement of a tolerant attitude toward other life is the very essence of liberalism.

Liberalism is needed both in social politics and in social morality but it is relatively more significant in the latter than in the former. It is, broadly speaking, a third of the force which enters into an adequate social politics and two thirds of an effective social morality. It plays a minor rôle, in other words, in the task of establishing the rough justice of a given equilibrium of power and a major rôle in perfecting the rough justice of politics into a decent social harmony between individuals in a community.

Though its rôle in social politics is a minor one it is nevertheless important. No old social system is supplanted purely by a conflict of interest between the privileged and the disinherited. The influence of the relatively disinterested, who view the struggle in rational and moral terms, is always considerable. No proletarian movement has yet existed that did not receive invaluable aid from middle-class intellectuals. The Negroes did not achieve their emancipation nor will they be able to gain further extensions of rights in our society without the aid of white men of sensitive conscience. The struggle for the full political and social emancipation of women was a contest of power in which the new economic weapons which an industrial civilization placed into the hands of women were probably decisive factors. The struggle was nevertheless not purely a contest of power. The women had the support of many men who had become convinced of the justice of the feminist cause.

Some of the morally inspired aid which is offered to the underdog in every social struggle is naturally mixed with egoistic motives. Consciously or unconsciously the idealists hope to preserve some traditional privileges through a policy of mitigating the most extravagant injustices of an old social system. This fact partially justifies the contempt of the radical for the "middle-class liberal." He is afraid that his moral idealism will confuse the issues and that it will fail to discern the fundamental realities of a social struggle.[1] On the other hand those who are driven by reason and conscience to espouse the cause of a social group other than their own are frequently more uncompromising than all but the most desperate of those who are driven by immediate interests. The uncompromising radicals in any social movement are the completely disinherited and the intellectual and religious idealists who have been forced by conscience to make common cause with them. For every Kerensky and Kropotkin there is a Lenin and a Trotsky and for every MacDonald and Snowden a Maxton and Fenner Brockway.

It is very important therefore, even in a period in which the political struggle is very obviously a contest of power, that the rational capacity to comprehend a total social situation should be extended. Every approximation of disinterestedness on the part of any large or small group in society gives strength to a cause which tradition outlaws but rational justice affirms. While liberalism has claimed too much for the force of reason in politics and has thus led to confusion, the radical claim that social issues are determined purely in terms of

[1]Leon Trotsky's analysis of the weaknesses of Prince Kropotkin's liberalism in the Russian revolutionary crisis and his excoriation of Kropotkin's drift toward reaction are interesting examples of the radical's recognition of the alloy in the attitudes of the moral idealist. See Trotsky, *History of the Russian Revolution*, Vol. II, pp. 178-79.

competing interests is too cynical to be true. It is belied by the very disinterestedness of the intellectual protagonists of a radical cause who make the claim.

The rational idealism which prompts men to espouse a cause other than their own is of a different quality from the type of rationality which seeks a way of harmony between conflicting causes. Perhaps it ought not to be placed in the category of liberal idealism because it is a fruit of the radical rather than the liberal spirit. Yet it does illustrate the power of rational or religious idealism as such and therefore belongs among those fruits of the spirit which radicals discount and liberals appreciate.

The contribution of the rational-liberal spirit is more important in the consolidation and stabilization of a political and social order than in its establishment; which is to say that it is more germane to the problems of social morality than to those of social politics. Suppressed rights must be asserted before even the idealists fully recognize them; but it is necessary that they be recognized and that fruitless conflict be avoided. If every new social standard had to be constantly defended by force of arms against those whose interests and convictions ran counter to it, society would be involved in an endless civil war. No wealthy class in any modern western nation has risen to the moral heights of demanding higher income taxes in order that the poor might have more adequate social services. Yet many wealthy people have acquiesced in such a new social standard, once they were confronted with a *fait accompli*. Such acquiescence has naturally not been a fruit of pure conscience. Fear of the consequences of political recalcitrance may have weighed as heavily in the balance as a moral recognition of the social rights of the underprivileged.

If the stakes are big enough and the prospects of defeating political opponents sufficiently promising, submission to a new social standard may actually be refused and the issue becomes joined in overt conflict. Nevertheless there is always the possibility that the ability to comprehend the needs of others, though not strong enough to initiate new social policies, will be strong enough to accept what has been accomplished. One may never hope that an entire class, group, or nation will voluntarily accept a new social situation which destroys old and cherished privileges. A measure of recalcitrance must always be dealt with by political force. But every degree of social imagination, by which the legitimacy of new and more equal forms of justice is recognized, reduces political tensions and the possibilities of conflict.

The liberal spirit is even more effective in reducing the frictions of an established order of society than in stabilizing a new order. No social order is conceivable in which basic conditions of justice will automatically make for harmonious human relations. Every social order of the future is bound to increase rather than diminish the intensity of social cohesion and thereby to accentuate the problems of aggregate living. No conceivable social order can exist without giving some men the power to order the lives of their fellowmen and thereby inviting them to use their power to their own advantage rather than the welfare of the whole. Human happiness must therefore always depend to a large degree upon the ability of men to adjust rights to rights and harmonize interests to interests with a minimum degree of tyranny, injustice and flagrant egoism.

While the typical individualistic liberal is inclined to give too much significance to the difference between a good slave-owner and a bad one and between a kind employer and a vexatious one, the difference for human happiness is very real; and no society will ever exist in which there will not be commensurate social relations where individual attitudes may not determine the happiness of the persons involved in it as much as the basic character of the relationship. This fact is rather obvious and needs to be stressed only because the typical radical fondly believes that a new type of social organization will automatically solve all social problems.

There will therefore always be a need in every society for a social pedagogy which knows how to extend the limits of human sympathy and increase the range of social imagination. The contributions of the liberal spirit to the problems of society, its fruits of tolerance, goodwill and rational sympathy are discounted in an era like our own because its claims have been too extravagant and its fruits have been too meagre for the task of building a new social order. But they will come into their own again in any established society which confronts the problems of minimizing racial antagonisms, of preserving harmony between social groups, of relating specialized social functions to each other and of making the relations between individuals in any social group tolerable.

XIX

RADICALISM AND RELIGIOUS DISINTERESTEDNESS

RADICALISM AND RELIGIOUS DISINTERESTEDNESS

THE liberal soul is pedestrian and uninspired. Its moral philosophy is always utilitarian and practical. It avoids the fanaticisms and passions of the servants of the absolute and goes about its business to tame life and bring larger and larger areas of human society into its circles of humane goodwill and prudent reciprocity. But liberalism can tame life only if it is fairly tame to begin with. It knows how to make life decent, intelligent and sociable in the comfortable atmosphere of a suburban village; and it is not unserviceable as the guiding genius of, say, an international conference on trade. In such an enterprise it softens prejudices and animosities and enhances mutual accord by considerations of prudence. But when life is not tame in the first instance, when it expresses itself in terms of tempest and fury and when it is driven by impulses arising from compelling immediate necessities or by dreams of the final good, by hunger or by sublime passion, the liberal soul is baffled and confused. It does not know what to do with life-as-nature, except, like the Lilliputians, spin gossamer threads around the giant and be surprised when the giant brushes its little restraints aside. Nor is it any more effective with life which yearns after the absolute and seeks by some heroic adventure or by some self-denying ordinance to burst the bounds of nature and find rest in pure spirit. The liberal soul produces neither warriors nor saints, heroes nor rebels, and it is ill at ease when confronted with their fury and their passion. The manifestations of life which reveal its darkest depths and its sublimest heights leave the liberal soul in baffled confusion. The prudent and shrewd calculations of its reason are unable to cope with life when it is totally unreasonable or when it strives with imprudent passion to achieve perfect rationality and purity. Confronted with a Lenin or a Napoleon on the one hand or a Francis or a Tolstoi on the other it can only deprecate their fanaticism and regret their ignorance of the principles of sociology.

Whenever reason aspires to something more than a manipulation of the immediate impulses and processes of society and seeks to achieve perfect purity and (in the field of morals) complete disinterestedness something of the religious spirit emerges. To understand the difference between the rationality of prudence which is completely involved in the play of impulse, though it seeks to direct it, and the unprudential passion for perfect rationality is to mark the distinction between a secular and a religious ethic. Whitehead indicates the distinction, though he does not apply it to the field of morals, in the words: "We have . . . two contrasted ways of considering reason. We can think of it as one among the operations involved in the existence of an animal body, and we can think of it in abstraction from any particular animal operations. . . . The older controversies have mainly to do with this latter mode of considering reason. For them, reason is the godlike faculty which surveys, judges and understands. In the newer controversy, reason is one of the items of operation implicated in the welter of the process. . . . There is reason, asserting itself above the world, and there is reason as one of many factors within the world. The Greeks have bequeathed to us two figures, whose real or mythical lives conform to these two notions— Plato and Ulysses. The one shares Reason with the Gods, and the other shares it with the foxes."[1]

When the passion for pure rationality expresses itself practically in the field of morals it issues in the demand for complete disinterestedness and insists that all life, rather than the life of the ego, be affirmed. The practical character of this demand transmutes rationality in morals into a spirituality which affects

[1] Alfred North Whitehead, *The Function of Reason*, p. 6.

and is affected by will and emotions. Pure rationality would be confined to the field of observation. If the effort is made to isolate the rational element in the field of moral life the tendency is always to set the reason against the emotions and to divide the human psyche. This tendency is particularly obvious in Stoic and Kantian morality. In the religious morality of Jesus reason is not set against the impulses. Reason accepts the altruism which is rooted in natural impulse and transmutes, perfects and enlarges it. The human psyche is not divided against itself in the attainment of the moral ideal. Altruistic impulse and rational imperatives are united in the will.

The observation of Jesus, "If ye love those who love you what thank have ye?" grows out of a spiritual insight in which natural altruistic emotions have been heightened by rational force. Yet to see life in its total relationships is not synonymous with feeling an obligation toward the whole of life. The sense of obligation arises only when life is not only seen but felt, when reason not only observes it from the outside but transmutes it from the inside. Pure rationality in morals is therefore more accurately described as pure spirituality. The entire spirit is engaged in the achievement of pure disinterestedness. The whole of life is seen and affirmed not merely by reason but by reason, emotion and will. The comprehension of life *per se* is an emotional as well as rational achievement because reason alone is incapable of achieving the synthesis of total reality, particularly living reality. Thus an adequate view of the whole must ultimately result in a religious appreciation of life as such in which the emotions of a living organism, which feels itself in organic contact with a living world, are combined with the more analytic insights of reason, which seeks to understand the details of this relationship.

The affirmation of all life is, even more than its comprehension, an achievement of the whole psyche and not simply of reason; for to affirm life in the absolute sense rather than the life of the ego means that the will (the total organization of personality) is extended beyond itself. The force of rationality always remains the primary source of this extension but it is an effective moral force only when it remains in organic contact with the whole. If it is separated it either becomes merely an observer of life or its demands are placed into such a contradiction to the impulses that the ideal of disinterestedness is unable to draw upon those resources of altruism which are supplied not by reason but by nature (mother-love, pity, gregariousness, etc.). The ideal of pure love and disinterestedness is therefore both a rational and religious ideal. Its form is possible only where reason comprehends life beyond itself in the most inclusive terms; but the obligation to realize the ideal represents a sublimation of the will and the emotions which is religious rather than rational in character.

The obligation of pure disinterestedness is clearly the universal moral obligation (expressed in every moral system which makes altruism morally preferable to egoism) raised to the highest degree. It represents the demands of pure spirit set against the immediate impulses of life. But since it is impossible to act in the world of nature and history in terms of pure spirit it is obvious that the highest moral ideal is compromised in every realization.

The paradox in which all morality moves is that nothing short of the affirmation of the total needs of humanity can be regarded as completely moral but that this can be accomplished concretely only by asserting the interests of those who have been defrauded against the interests of those who have undue privileges. Every practical assertion of the principle of disinterestedness therefore involves the assertion of interest. It is idle to deny that the assertion of neglected interests may not lead to an undue emphasis upon them and thus betray disinterestedness. The problem of all practical morality is therefore that of revealing the spirit of justice and disinterestedness in actual life without compromising too seriously with the forces egoism and interest which express themselves in all history.

The solution of asceticism for this problem falls clearly into the category of morbid perfectionism. In asceticism the demands of pure spirit express themselves in terms so individualistic that the organic relation of the individual to society is destroyed and his perfection becomes parasitic on the "sins" of those who continue to assume responsibility for the larger relations of life. Ascetic disinterestedness is not only an irrelevance from the standpoint of the needs of an adequate social morality but it is finally self-defeating from the standpoint of its own goal. The mystic-ascetic effort to destroy egoism involves the soul in greater and greater preoccupation with the self.

The solution of orthodox Christianity is hardly less satisfactory. The validity of the absolute ideal is recognized but it is changed into a purely religious rather than ethical ideal. The tension between egoism and the obligation of disinterestedness is therefore transferred from the field of morals to that of religion. This tempts orthodox Christianity to make premature compromises with the inequalities and injustices of an established social order and to regard the assertion of neglected social interests as more sinful than the assertion of established interests. The resource of the orthodox position is that it provides insights by which the imperfections of every concrete social achievement are recognized.

In rational liberalism the demands of absolute love and disinterestedness are reduced to a prudent and utilitarian altruism. The value and inevitability of this emphasis have been previously considered. Its weakness lies in the fact that its rational disinterestedness either escapes to the vantage point of pure observation upon life (in which case it has similarities with asceticism) or it becomes involved in the play of impulse and interest without seriously checking individual or collective egoism. It is cursed by either timidity or hypocrisy. A rational-liberal adjustment of interest to interest usually means a measured but insufficient check upon the interests of the group from which the idealism proceeds. Aristotle, who is in many respects the fountain source of all liberal morals, was thus able to elaborate a political theory in which slavery and the caste system of Greek society were completely rationalized and justified. It is interesting to note that the equalitarian and universalistic elements in morality were much stronger in Stoicism than in Aristotle and the difference between the two may be due to the fact that Stoicism was a religio-rational morality. The implications of the moral ideal were therefore pressed more rigorously to their logical conclusion.

The tendency of modern liberalism to justify the interests of the socially privileged in the very act of seeming to consider the interests of all groups in im-

partial survey is illustrated in journalism of the type
of Walter Lippmann's. Here suave and bland pre-
tenses of disinterestedness seek, with no great success, to hide a definite protagonism of the viewpoint
of the present financial and industrial oligarchy.
Christian liberalism, leaning on secular liberalism
more than it realizes, is frequently tempted to the
same sin. Its errors are doubly reprehensible because
it appropriates the prestige of the religiously inspired absolute ethic of Jesus for the ideals of prudence which have developed in a commercial civilization.

Judged in terms both of its inner integrity and its
social consequences a radical social ethic is the most
effective manifestation of the religious and moral
ideal of disinterestedness. The religious drive toward
the absolute in it prevents it from suggesting merely
slight modifications in the unequal social relations of
a given social order in the name of the ideal of justice. On the contrary it sets the absolute ideal of
equal justice into sharp and vivid juxtaposition to
the injustices and inequalities of society. This policy is clearly a fruit of the religio-rational demand
that all life be equally affirmed. Considerations of
prudence and the practical necessities of a social
order always relativize the ideal of equal justice and
prove that it cannot be fully attained. This fact
would seem to justify the liberal rather than the

radical as the more practical statesman. But it also proves that the radical is superior in religious and spiritual insight. His ideal is in fact akin to the religious ideal of pure love. Both are unattainable and yet every historic moral and social achievement must be judged in their light.

The ideal of equal justice sets the demands of pure spirit against the facts of nature. Nature does not endow men equally; and the impulses of nature create societies in which inequalities of endowment are accentuated because the shrewd and the strong are able to arrogate powers and privileges which enhance their strength and place the weak, the simple and the unfortunate under additional disadavantages. Every social system thus tends to create differences in strength and weakness, in wealth and poverty much greater than anything which the world of pure nature knows. Every social system endows the strong man, who is able to grasp the reins of power, with strength which is derived from society itself and is not of his own contriving. Thus the human world suffers from inequalities such as the brute world does not know.

The fact that this will be a perennial problem in every social system may prove the Marxian radical wrong in assuming that a collectivist society will finally eliminate every basis of injustice. But he is not wrong in setting the absolute demands of justice against the inequalities of the present social order nor in believing that the destruction of present disproportions of economic power through collective ownership will make for a more equal justice.

The religious character of this demand for equal justice is attested by the whole history of religion. While religion may make its demands so absolute that it despairs of realizing them in history there has always been a strain in religious thought which has insisted that love and equal justice be realized in history. Whenever religious idealism directs itself to the problems of history it dreams of the day when the mighty will be cast from their seats and those of low degree exalted, when, in other words, disproportions of power will be levelled.

If the effort is made to achieve this result in political terms, when, in other words, religious apocalypticism is changed into a political program, it becomes immediately apparent that it is no longer an expression of pure disinterestedness. As soon as a moral criticism of the undue privileges of a few becomes associated with a political policy it demands that the interests of the many be asserted against the few. There is always a possibility that in this assertion of interest against interest neglected values and interests be asserted too narrowly. Thus for instance the proletarian may neglect the legitimate interests and override the natural desires of the agrarian poor.

Or both may express their protest against injustice in such vindictive terms that the highest values of society are imperilled. The dangers of corruption in radical disinterestedness are, in other words, important from the standpoint of an adequate social morality and the desire to avoid them is dictated by something more legitimate than a morbid individual perfectionism.

The dangers cannot be completely avoided in any social morality which assumes political responsibility. An organic relation to socio-political movements involves every disinterested spirit in the forces of nature which express themselves in the political world. Lest moral perfectionists become too concerned about that problem it is well to point out that every one (with the possible exception of the ascetic) is equally involved in the play of natural forces in politics. For the next decades those who desire to make a moral choice between the semi-moral alternatives of politics must make a choice between hypocrisy and vengeance. The old world which hides its injustices behind the forms of justice is embattled with a new world which expresses its protest against injustice in vindictive terms. Purer moral insights may mitigate the hypocrisy of the old order and the vengeance of the new. But they cannot eliminate these evils completely nor avoid all the perils which lurk in them. A choice has to be made and it ought to be fairly clear on which side the moralist who aspires to disinterestedness must cast his fortunes. Even when the rebels and martyrs of the radical cause are involved in the animosities of the social conflict they reveal, at their best, authentic proofs of their kinship with the children of the spirit. It must be admitted of course that radical disinterestedness may become completely engulfed by the forces of nature in history which it seeks to manipulate. It may express itself in terms so vindictive and so blind a hatred that it becomes a peril to society and to the interests of those it seeks to serve. There are always demonic forces in politics. To seek their complete elimination is a counsel of perfection. It is nevertheless important that they be restrained by those who seek to use them for moral ends.

It is necessary for this reason that radical spirituality be brought under the scrutiny of the more absolute demands and the higher perspectives which are characteristic of classical religion. The most courageous and honest effort to establish justice in history must remain under the discipline of pure spirit through which the imperfections of every historical achievement are recognized and the perils to society in every assertion of interest against interest are discovered. This is a fact which modern radicalism is bound to treat with scorn. Its utopianism makes it incapable of recognizing the relativities in its moral attitudes and the possibilities of new tyrannies and injustices in its policies. Those who have looked more deeply into the problems of the human spirit and human society must not be deterred by this scorn from insisting that radical disinterestedness will become completely corrupted and a peril to its own ends if it cannot maintain contact with the spiritual disciplines through which the perils of anarchy and tyranny in every political movement are discovered.

A moral perspective which is high enough to discover the perils and relativities in every historic movement naturally makes demands which are not capable of complete realization in history. Pure spirit in man always suggests a realm of reality which transcends the realm of nature. It creates tensions which cannot be completely resolved in moral endeavor. Some way must be found to relax these tensions without destroying the validity of the absolute ideal or without tempting too premature compromises with historical forces. Whenever the tension between spirit and nature is fully felt the æsthetic motif in religion arises to compete with the ethical urge. Men find it necessary not only to approximate perfection ethically but to adjust themselves to an imperfect world in terms of æsthetic insights which, in classical religion, are expressed in the experience of grace. There is no place in either radical or liberal utopianism for the "experience of grace."

The hope of realizing perfection in history has made such an experience unnecessary. When the hard realities of history have once again dissipated the utopian dreams of the present the emphasis of classical religion upon the experience of grace will find its way back again into the moral and religious life of the race.

XX

THE ASSURANCE OF GRACE

XX

THE ASSURANCE OF GRACE

WHENEVER the tension between spirit and nature is adequately maintained and the imperatives of spirit are pressed rigorously against the immediate impulses of nature, the result is not only a morality of purer disinterestedness but a religion of grace which seeks to console the human spirit to its inevitable defeat in the world of nature and history. It is significant that in the Christian religion, Jesus, who in his own life incarnated the spirit of pure love to a unique and remarkable degree, became for Paul the symbol and revelation of a divine forgiveness which knew how to accept human intentions for achievements. The relation of the religion of Jesus to that of Paul is a perfect illustration of the relation of a religious morality of pure disinterestedness to a supra-moral religion of grace. The force of the same religious urge is revealed in both of them.

A high religion creates both disinterestedness and the realization that pure love and disinterestedness are impossible of achievement. It declares on the one hand, "Be ye therefore perfect even as your

Father in heaven is perfect," and on the other it confesses, "Why callest thou me good; no one is good save God." The same rigor which discovers the inertia of natural impulse sufficiently to make a high morality possible also reveals the resistance of nature to spirit so clearly that the demands of pure spirit are seen to be frustrated in nature and history. Pure religion is thus at the same time the inspiration of a high morality and a consolation for the frustrations which moral purpose faces in history.

The consolations of the assurance of grace in religious faith have no meaning to the modern man and the modern spirit because the modern spirit is still under the illusion that the logic of the spirit needs only to be recognized to be fulfilled. For it life is a simple process in which spirit gains ever more impressive victories over natural impulse; its optimistic monism is too thoroughgoing and there are not enough dualistic elements in its thought for an adequate ethic or religion. The naturalistic monism of modern culture is possible both because the ethical character of the forces of nature is overestimated and because the rigor of the ethical demand is softened by prudential qualifications. This superficial monism is destroyed whenever ethical passion rises to a pitch where prudence is discarded or when philosophical and religious penetration discloses life in both its heights and depths. It may be claimed therefore that religion and morality are related to each other in terms of mutual support; a profound religion makes a pure ethical passion possible and a pure ethical passion makes religion necessary.

In the religion of Jesus ethical tension and relaxation from tension through the assurance of grace are curiously intermingled so that the latter does not become a peril to the former. This is less true of the religion of Paul, and the Christian orthodoxy which is derived from it. In Paul the dualism and pessimism are more consistently and philosophically developed and the chasm between nature and God must therefore be bridged by a more specific act of divine grace, which for Paul and Christian orthodoxy is to be found in the historic incarnation and redemption. In Jesus the mythology which expresses his thought is much more paradoxical and unphilosophical and he is therefore more able to do justice both to the tension required for an adequate ethic and the release from tension necessary to an adequate religion.

Essentially the experience of grace in religion is the apprehension of the absolute from the perspective of the relative. The unachieved is in some sense felt to be achieved or realized. The sinner is "justified" even though his sin is not overcome. The world, as revealed in its processes of nature, is known to be imperfect and yet it is recognized as a creation of God. Man is regarded as both a sinner and a child of

God. In these paradoxes true religion makes present reality bearable even while it insists that God is denied, frustrated and defied in the immediate situation.

In Jesus' religio-poetic conceptions of life and the world the impartiality of nature, which to the humanist represents nature's injustice and indicates her inability to support the moral values conceived by man, is regarded as a revelation of divine mercy which "maketh his sun to rise on the evil and the good and sendeth rain on the just and the unjust." The conception here is of a God who, in spite of his transcendence, does not negate the forces of nature but reveals himself in them. Here religious faith transmutes nature's unconcern for the moral distinctions between human good and evil into a revelation of the highest spiritual achievement: forgiving love. The very pinnacle of the spirit is found in the broad basis of natural process. The whole world process is endowed with spiritual meaning which reveals both the judgments and the mercy of God. In this imaginative insight the relation of the assurance of forgiveness to the demand for perfection in high religion is revealed at its best. Nothing in conceptions of orthodox and conventional religion approaches this profundity.

In the same way Jesus finds glimpses of God, of pure spirit, of perfect love, in human nature, in the love of parents for their children for instance and in the innocency of little children; yet he also knew that out of the heart of this same human nature "proceed evil thoughts, murders, adulteries, fornications, thefts, false witness, blasphemies." His confidence in the goodness of human nature is not as simple as that of liberal Christianity. The kingdom of God, in his view, will be established not by the goodness of loving men but by the grace of God. Yet there are glimpses of the eternal and the absolute in human nature.

The relation of ethical tension and religious relaxation is perhaps most perfectly revealed in the beatitudes of Jesus in which bliss is promised to the unsatisfied. The knowledge and the certainty of God are a gift to, and an achievement of, those who strive after perfection without the illusion of having attained it, the "poor in spirit," and those who "hunger and thirst after righteousness." Those who imagine themselves righteous are consistently condemned. Those who strive after pure spirit are consoled in the inevitable frustration which attends their striving because in their very search after perfection they are initiated into the true character of spirit and realize that perfection is love and not justice. Thus they obtain mercy while they learn to be merciful.

The contrite recognition of the imperfections in the self further reduces the strain of living in an imperfect world because it reduces the presumptions and demands which the soul makes upon the world and upon its fellowmen. When the evils from which men suffer are recognized as having their root in sins which the self shares with all mankind they are borne more patiently and with less resentment than would otherwise be the case. In the mythology of Genesis, even the inadequacies of nature are ascribed to the sin of man, a somewhat too simple solution for the problem of evil, but one which does credit to man's moral imagination.

It must be immediately evident that every religious assurance of grace and every concomitant emotion of contrition contain certain perils to a socio-moral passion which strives to correct the imperfections of society and which must count upon impatient and, on the whole, self-righteous men to perform the task. The knowledge of the equal sinfulness of all human nature is not completely compatible with a social purpose which sets the relatively good ideal against the relative injustices of society. This incompatibility between the temper of classical religion and strenuous morality proves that the relation of religion and morality is never simple and is not exhausted in their mutual support of each other on certain levels. In certain areas the conflict is permanent; but its permanency does not justify the suppression of one in favor of the other.

All men who live with any degree of serenity live by

some assurance of grace. In every life there must at least be times and seasons when the good is felt as a present possession and not as a far-off goal. The sinner must feel himself "justified," that is, he must feel that his imperfections are understood and sympathetically appreciated as well as challenged. Whenever he finds himself in a circle of love where he is "completely known and all forgiven" something of the mercy of God is revealed to him and he catches a glimpse of the very perfection which has eluded him. Perhaps the most sublime insight of Jewish prophets and the Christian gospel is the knowledge that since perfection is love, the apprehension of perfection is at once the means of seeing one's imperfection and the consoling assurance of grace which makes this realization bearable. This ultimate paradox of high religion is not an invention of theologians or priests. It is constantly validated by the most searching experiences of life.

It is a literal fact that the processes of nature and history are revelations of grace as well as of judgment. Logically every life deserves destruction. Since it is predatory either individually or collectively, it ought to die at the hands of those it has exploited. Though it may perish in the end, the God of history and nature is truly longsuffering, "slow to anger and plenteous in mercy." If, for instance, the white man were to expiate his sins committed against

285

the darker races, few white men would have the right to live. They live, partly because they are strong enough to maintain themselves against their enemies and partly because their enemies have not taken vengeance upon them. They survive, in other words, both by the law of nature and by the law of grace. That is why the same facts of history lend themselves both to cynical and to religious interpretations.

The religious imagination sees truly when it regards the slow processes of history and the impartialities of nature as revelations of divine mercy. The same radiant morning sun may dispel the stupor of the man who has spent the night in a drunken orgy and call the diligent husbandman to his daily tasks. That aspect of nature is just as significant as the fact that the same wintry storm may "destroy both good and bad alike." If in the latter case nature seems to be inframoral in her judgments it is not wrong to discover supramoral justice (mercy) in the former case. Thus vital religion catches glimpses of ultimate perfection in the very imperfections of man and history. Only a very rational religion relegates perfection completely to another world of pure transcendence. The modern Barthian emphasis on "the qualitative difference between time and eternity" has much more in common with Greek Platonism than with the paradoxical religion of Jesus.

The experience of grace has been stereotyped

286

by religious orthodoxy and made to depend upon the dispensations of religious institutions, the acceptance of dogmas and upon faith in the efficacy of grace in specific facts of history (revelation and incarnation).

The fact that Christian orthodoxy relates and fastens the experience of grace, which in the religion of Jesus is organically related to the total moral and religious experience in human life, to the one fact of the incarnation need not lead to a magical and unmoral interpretation of grace. Religious faith needs specific symbols; and the Jesus of history is a perfect symbol of the absolute in history because the perfect love to which pure spirit aspires is vividly realized in the drama of his life and cross. Thus a man becomes the symbol of God and the religious sense that the absolute invades the relative and the historical is adequately expressed. Naturally rational theology has difficulty in bringing the paradoxes of this mythological conception into the canons of rationality. In both orthodox and liberal theology the profound mythological conceptions of the incarnation and atonement are rationalized and their profundity is endangered by canons of logic and consistency.

In orthodoxy it is feared that some human imperfection and some relativity of history may still cling to the symbol of the absolute because the symbol is historical, a man living in Galilee and speaking the language of a particular time and place. These relativities are rigorously effaced or obscured by the insistence that Christ was "the Only Begotten Son of God; Begotten of his Father before all the Worlds, God of God, Light of Light, Very God of Very God, Begotten not made, Being of one substance with the Father." The modern mind may find little plausibility in such a confession but it is quite consistent with a dualistic world-view which is unable to find the absolute and perfect in the nature of the historic and the relative.

Unfortunately the consistent dualism of orthodoxy complicates the task, necessary to the original meaning of the mythology, of relating the absolute to history. It does not adequately express the deeper feelings of the human spirit which knows itself to be a citizen of two worlds, the world of spirit and the world of nature, which knows these two worlds to be at war with each other but also believes that there is some ultimate resolution and reconciliation in the conflict. The long controversy about the two natures of Christ in the history of Christian theology represents the futile effort of reason to comprehend or to define the mythological absurdities and profundities of the original myth. It is both interesting and pathetic that the dualism of Christian orthodoxy should be finally stated in its most consistent terms in our own day in reaction to Christian liberalism and that the dialectical theology (Barthianism) which draws these final pessimistic and dualistic conclusions should find no meaning in history or nature except as the one event in history (the incarnation) illumines the scene. It is significant too that this one event in history really ceases to be an event in history and that the symbol of the absolute never really becomes incarnate.

Against this kind of consistent dualism and pessimism Christian liberalism seems to have a more plausible rationalism. It believes that the Jesus of history was a symbol of the absolute because he personifies "the highest human values." The goodness of human nature and finally the ethical character of history itself are thus the revelations of the absolute. If this seems more plausible and rational to our day than the position of Christian orthodoxy it is only because our culture has been an optimistic one and it has not realized what frustrations and defeats the spirit meets in the impulses of nature and history.

In consistent orthodoxy the absolute and the relative, the divine and human, the spiritual and the natural are so completely separated that the ultimate faith of religion in the meaningfulness of life rests upon one event in history which is not truly historical. Religion is thus reduced to magic. In liberal theology on the other hand the tension between spirit and nature is not fully recognized and all history and nature (including human nature) are consequently invested prematurely with the aura of the absolute and the perfect. In both cases rationalism has destroyed the original mythological profundity of the Christian religion which sought to express the idea that the conflict between spirit and nature is a real conflict, that no complete victory of spirit in history is possible, but that defeat is turned into victory when the unachieved perfection is discovered to be a forgiving love which justifies (understands) man's imperfection.

Every effort to state the idea of the grace and forgiveness of God in purely rational terms suffers from the same difficulties encountered in stating the conception of the relation of God to the world. The idea of grace can be stated adequately only in mythical terms. In the mythos of Jesus the holy God reveals his holiness in terms of mercy and this mercy redeems the sinner. This redemption means that the sinner knows himself to be in the embrace of divine love in spite of his sin. The holiness of God thus creates both the consciousness of sin and the consolation which makes the consciousness of sin bearable.

When put in rational terms this experience means that the man who is involved in the relativities of the natural and historical process finds himself nevertheless in contact with the final and the absolute life which is above the process. Thus the tension between the absolute and the relative is overcome. But the rationalization of the mythos robs it of some of its significance. In purely rational terms the sin of man becomes merely the imperfection and relativity inherent in the process of history and the sense of personal responsibility for evil actions is lost. Since in every human life the egoism of natural impulse is actually transmuted into a willful conflict of life with life the mythos of the fall and sin therefore does justice to the actual facts which a rational conception of human imperfection fails to reveal. But a rational conception not only blunts the idea of evil as sin into an idea of evil as imperfection: it also transmutes the apprehension of perfection into an experience which threatens to remove the concept of imperfection. Thus the sinner who is "justified" feels himself to have attained perfection. If on the other hand a rational effort is made to avoid the dangers of this confusion of perfection and imperfection it results in a dualism of which Neo-Platonism is a typical example and in which the ethical distinctions between good and evil are lost in metaphysical distinctions between the world of pure form and of concrete reality. Christian orthodoxy derived from Paul is very frequently close to errors of Neo-Platonic dualism. Christian liberalism on the other hand falls into the monistic errors of rationalism and fails to develop either a conception of sin for which grace is really required or yet a conception of grace which maintains the idea of the sinfulness and imperfection of the world as it illumines the imperfect world with the aura of the absolute and perfect. The experience of grace, in short, can only be expressed in mythological terms if it is not to become a peril to the ethical life. For only in the concepts of religious myth can an imperfect world mirror the purposes of a divine Creator and can the mercy of God make the fact of sin and imperfection bearable without destroying moral responsibility for the evil of imperfection or obscuring its realities in actual history.

Ideally the Christian religion therefore is rooted in a mythology which does justice both to the necessity for moral tension in life and the need for the relaxation of this tension. Practically the Christianity of the churches has subordinated ethical tension to the assurance of grace or (as in the case of liberal Christianity) it has destroyed ethical tension by a too monistic and naturalistic mythology. If ethical tension has been maintained it has expressed itself, in both orthodoxy and liberalism, in too purely individualistic terms so that the moral vigor which is most relevant to the urgent moral problems of an era which must deal with the life and death of social systems is expressed outside the churches. It comes to its completest expression among those who have learned in bitter experience how real the conflict between spirit and nature is in history.

The radical idealists who express this moral vigor in the modern day are so completely immersed in the specific problems which face them that they can hardly be expected to do justice to the perennial problems of the human spirit or to know that a relative victory over evil, however important, is not the final victory. When the storms and fevers of this era are passed and modern civilization has achieved a social system which provides some basic justice compatible with the necessities of a technical age the perennial problems of humanity will emerge once more. Religious insights which seem for the moment to be inimical to moral progress and moral vigor will come into their own again. There will be unjust men in this new society of justice; and good men will feel that they are not as just as they ought to be. The perils of nature and the inhumanities of man will continue to take their toll in human life. Men's hopes will be shattered by untoward fortune; family circles will be invaded by death and widows and orphans will seek not only security from society but some faith in the meaning of life which will make the chaos of the moment bearable; good will still be turned into evil when the devotion of naïvely virtuous men is sluiced by the design of knaves and the ignorance of fools into ignoble causes and dangerous channels; men will continue in short to find the promptings of the spirit frustrated by the forces of nature within

293

them and the hopes of the spirit shattered by the forces of nature about them. They will suffer both at the hands of nature and at the hands of man and they will find the semi-conscious cruelties of conscious men more difficult to bear than "the trampling march of unconscious power."

When these problems of man in nature and man in society are seen again as perennial problems of the human spirit, and not merely as injustices of an era, men will have to learn once more that though evil must be resisted there are limits to the possibility of resistance and some evil must be borne. The weak will cry out against the injustices of the strong and they will confront the eternal problem of how to prevent bitterness from corroding their spirit and spoiling the purity of their testimonies. Men will learn that nature can never be completely tamed to do man's will. Her blind caprices, her storms and tempests will continue, on occasion, to brush aside man's handiwork as a housewife destroys a cobweb; and her inexorable processes will run counter to men's hopes and designs. Then men will see again the importance of accommodating the vision of perfection to an imperfect world without losing the urge to perfect the world. In order to do that they must find suggestions of meaning in chaos and glimpses of ultimate perfection within imperfection.

The inevitable imperfections of life and history

will be borne with the greater serenity if the ego recognizes that the blind forces of nature which frustrate the spirit are in the self as well as outside it. In classical Christianity it is suggested again and again that repentance is the beginning of redemption, even that it is synonymous with redemption. This is a profound insight; for the evils and frustrations of life and history would be, in fact, unbearable if contrition did not reduce the presumptions and pretensions of the self and reveal the fact that some of the confusions from which the spirit suffers have their direct source in the chaos of the self and that others may be regarded as punishment for the sins of the self even if they have not been obviously caused by them. The consciousness of sin in classical religion is closely related to the cynic's interpretation of human nature; but it is never purely pessimistic. Classical religious faith is always saved from despair because it knows that sin is discovered by the very faith through which men catch a glimpse of the reality of spirit. Both the heights and the depths of the world of spirit are known. The knowledge of the depths within the self saves from pride, prevents a bitter criticism of the sins of others and makes a sullen rebellion against the imperfections of nature and history impossible; the knowledge of the heights keeps profound self-knowledge from degenerating into bitter disillusionment.

These religious insights guarantee the ethically striving soul a measure of serenity and provide the spiritual relaxation without which all moral striving generates a stinking sweat of self-righteousness and an alternation of fanatic illusions and fretful disillusionments. Naturally it is not easy to preserve a decent balance between the ethical urge to realize perfection in history and the religious need of reconciliation with imperfection. In particular periods of history the one will devour the other. Sometimes the ethical urge will degenerate into an illusion-crammed ethical utopianism; at other times religious insights will betray the soul into a premature peace with and transcendence over the world's imperfections. But the human spirit will always discover in time that sanity and wholesomeness are possible only when two partially incompatible and partially supplementary attitudes toward life are both embraced and espoused. Then it will find its way back to the profound mythologies which do justice to both; and it will disavow not only the moribund religion which solves the problem of the spirit in nature by magic but also the superficial rational moralism which dreams of gaining a quick and easy victory of the spirit over nature.

INDEX

INDEX

America, bourgeois republic of, 69; capitalism in, 72, 77, 79, 81, 83; proletariat in, 160. *See also* Chap. VI, *The Social Struggle in America.*

Angell, Norman, 46.

Apocalypticism, 125 f., 271; of Christianity and Marxism, 132 ff.; of Jesus, 212, 214.

Aristotle, 40, 268.

Asceticism, 35, 110 f., 179, 266 f., 272; relation of to religion, 7.

Barbarism, 44, 141 f., 165 f., 174; of Fascism, 188. *See also* Chap. XI, *The Executors of Judgment. See also* Chap. XIII, *The Peril of Barbarism in the Spirit of Vengeance.*

Barthianism, 286, 288 f.; pessimism of, 289.

Benda, Julien, 201 f.

Buddhism, pessimism of, 202, 211.

Calvinism, 130, 222.

Capitalism, 12 f., 24–27, 79 ff., 87; as self-destroying, 121, 127; decline of, 18, 28, 56, 59; in America, 72, 77, 83; in England, 51, 72; in Germany, 72; state capitalism in America, 79, 81; unethical character of modern, 30.

Carlyle, A. J., 218 *n.*, 219 *n.*

Chase, Stuart, 46, 53.

Christianity, 92, 193, 200, 279; dualism of orthodox, 203 ff., 213, 217; individualism of, 107 f.; Liberal, 113, 135, 213, 289 f., 292; mythology of, 93, 124 ff., 201; optimism of Liberal, 203 f., 283; orthodox, 135 f., 209, 213 f., 216 f., 225, 267, 281, 287–92, 295 f.; pessimism of orthodox, 108, 111, 202 ff., 213, 218–22, 224, 231; political realism of orthodox, 210, 211–4, 220 f.; sanctification of social and political ills in orthodox, 217–22. *See also* Chap. XV, *The Political Realism of Christian Orthodoxy. See also* Chap. XIV, *The Conflict between Christianity and Communism.*

Churchill, Winston, 118.

Civilization, anarchy of modern, 45 f.; as affecting the family, 100 ff.; commercial and industrial nature of modern, 3 f., 10, 25 ff., 65, 72, 74, 159; individual in modern, 115 f.; mechanical nature of, 3 f., 14 f., 70, 93 f., 99, 159, 196, 239. *See also* Chap. I, *The Life and Death of Civilizations. See also* Chap. VII, *The Virtues of a Bourgeois Civilization.*

Class Struggle, 15 f. *See also* Chap. VI, *The Social Struggle in America.*

Communism, 88, 93, 140, 167 ff., 171, 185–9; as product of rational and mechanical civilization, 94, 102, 196; concept of the family in, 102 f.; emphasis upon catastrophe, 177, 195; illusions of, 244, 270; in Russia, 171–4, 185, 245 f.; religious element in, 193, 203, 230. *See also* Chap. XIV, *The*

299

300

251, 253 f., 258, 261 f., 267 f.;
as related to asceticism 110;
Christian, 113, 135, 269, 289
ff.; illusions of, 136, 178 f.,
237; individualism of, 107,
116; in economic theory and
reform, 53. *See also* Chap.
XVIII, *The Liberal Spirit in
Morals.*
Lippmann, Walter, 269.
Locke, John, 91, 93.
Love, ideal of pure, 114, 212 ff.,
219, 233, 265, 270.
Luther, Martin, 41, 219.

MacDonald, J. Ramsay, 81, 254.
Marx, Karl, 128 f.
Marxism, 144, 167 ff., 177, 181,
187 ff.; catastrophism of, 177,
195; illusions of, 244, 270;
mythology of, 120–136. *See
also* Chap. X, *Mythology and
History. See also* Chap. XIII,
*The Peril of Barbarism in
the Spirit of Vengeance. See
also* Chap. XIV, *The Conflict
between Christianity and
Communism. See also* Com-
munism.
McIlwain, C. H., 220 *n.*
Mechanism, of modern civiliza-
tion, 4, 69, 70, 113. *See also*
Civilization.
Mediævalism, 66 f., 70.
Mennonites, the, 11 f., 134.
Mill, J. S., 113.
Mythology, 198, 200; of Chris-
tianity, 93, 123 ff., 201; of
Communism, 126–36, 193; of
progress, 123. *See also* Chap.
X, *Mythology and History.*

Nature, impulse of, 9, 114 f.,
124, 136, 140, 143, 171, 198 f.,
230, 262 f., 270, 286, 288 ff.,
293 f.; in politics, 118, 279 f.
Negroes, the, 253.
Neo-Platonism, 291.

Optimism, in estimate of human
nature, 111; of bourgeois naturalism, 194, 199, 203; of

communism, 194, 214, 224; of
Liberal Christianity, 203, 214;
of modern civilization, 3 f.,
17; of rationalists and liberals, 29 ff., 31, 33 f., 39, 45 ff.,
110, 214.

Patriotism, attitude of radical
toward, 180 ff.
Peasant, the, 175, 186 ff., 271;
fascist tendencies of, 171, 188;
individualism of, 186 f.; in
Russian Communism, 169, 172
f., 175 ff., 243 f.
Pessimism, as factor in religion
of communism, 195 f., 203; of
asceticism, 110 ff.; of Barthianism, 289; of Buddhism,
203, 311; of Christian orthodoxy, 108, 111, 202 f., 213 f.,
218, 222, 224, 231; of profound religion, 195 ff.
Proletariat, the, 78, 141 f., 148,
161 f., 167 ff., 171, 175, 271;
in America, 160. *See also*
Communism. *See also* Marxism.
Proudhon, 128.
Psyche, the, 265. *See also* Spirituality.

Quakers, the, 111 f.

Radicalism, 251; utopianism of,
273. *See also* Chap. XVI, *A
Radical Political Theory. See
also* Chap. XIX, *Radicalism
and Religious Disinterestedness.*
Rathenau, Walter, 45.
Rationalism, at work in Christian theologies, 289 ff.; idealism of, 67, 254 f.; illusions of,
16, 29 ff., 39, 45–48, 93 f., 113,
115, 140.
Reason, 4–9, 254, 262–5; age of,
67. *See also* Rationalism.
Reformation, the, 66.
Religion, 7 f., 10, 14, 92, 114,
170, 193–205; classical and
"high," 273 ff., 279–82, 284 ff.;
attitude of Communism to-